RECESSION PROOF

BUSINESS

A Time Tested Battle Plan For Tough Economies

DISCLAIMER

This book and its author make no guarantee regarding your business success or failure. The word "proof" used in the title and herein throughout this book is to be defined as "improving in resilience" and is not to imply any form of "immunity" or otherwise being "immune" to recessionary market forces.

No business is "immune" to market conditions and the author makes no claim that the content of this book will create immunity to such. The contents of this book are solely intended to offer information about improving business resiliency.

Use of the information provided in this book is at your own risk and benefit. No warranty is provided or made.

Links provided throughout the book are informational in nature. The author may receive financial compensation as an affiliate for purchases made through linked websites.

Published in Boise, Idaho by Made Easy Brands.

Made Easy Brands books may be purchased for educational, business, or sales promotional use. For information and other inquiries, such as speaking inquiries or bulk order purchase options, please e-mail hello@madeeasybrands.com.

Printed in the United States of America

1st edition, January 2023

ISBN: 978-1-7366796-4-7 (paperback)

CONTENTS

INTRODUCTION
Winter Is Not Coming.
It Has Already Arrived.

RECESSION PROOF

INTRODUCTION

You are smarter than the average squirrel in the forest...

Congratulations!

Most squirrels (aka. business owners) wait until winter is at its worst before they attempt to resupply their stash. You, on the other hand, are a go-getter; getting ahead of the decreased supply that winter brings by actioning early and gathering all the best nuts (customers) before others realize what you're doing. Smart.

No doubt, that is why you've picked up this book. You see the storm brewing and want to get ahead of the craziness that is bound to ensue.

In what will seem like no time flat, the other squirrels are going to start getting, well, squirrelly. Rational thought will give way to irrational desperation as the snow begins to fall and what was once a green and prosperous forest... freezes.

The time to act is now. Well, actually, it was yesterday, but today will do just fine. You're still ahead of the game when compared to the others simply because you've picked up this book.

What, exactly, should you be actioning on, though? It's likely a question that you're asking yourself. Even more likely is that it's the sole reason you chose this book out of the thousands available to you. You chose well.

This book shall be your guide to where to find, collect, and store the best nuts. How to take a good nut and make it better. And, how to get the most out of the lot that you've collected.

Before we get to all of that, though, a sports analogy. Because, well, it turns out that, even though you're ahead of the other squirrels, you're still behind the curve of where you _really_ should be.

In all honesty, and I am sorry to tell you this so bluntly... <u>you have arrived late to the most important game of your life.</u>

The other players are already on the field. The stadium is packed, and the crowd is roaring. The ref, standing at mid-field with whistle perched between two angrily puckered lips, is ready to get the show on the road.

RECESSION PROOF

All eyes are staring intently…at you.

It's go time.

But this will be a battle unlike any you've ever faced. On turf unfamiliar to you. With rules that you do not yet know.

It will be a battle for your business, for its very survival. One where the losers will be many, and the winners will take all. Mercy will not be granted. The merciless will prevail.

There will be no bailout from the powers above, and for the first time since the 1930's, the victors must _earn_ their winnings.

You might feel the sweat of nervous anticipation beading on your brow for what you know is ahead of you. Butterflies fluttering in your belly. Adrenaline flowing through your veins. Simultaneously, you might feel both powerful and weak. Knees buckling, yet quads amped for battle.

In this very moment in time, you are faced with a choice. Will you pivot on your back foot, take what is yours, and run to safety far away from the game of business? Or, will you put your chips on the table, betting everything you have invested – every dollar, every minute, every sacrifice?

Of course, the answer here is already known. You've never been one to let fear get the better of you. You are cunning, sharp, and determined. Some may even call you stubborn. A little rocky economic cycle won't shake you off course.

But you also recognize that you'll need every advantage you can get on this new field of business battle. And that is why you have found yourself here, hands grasping paper, eyes shifting from side to side, brain moving a mile a minute. You know that it is now or never. You've known for a while now. You're hoping this book will shortcut you to victory.

So, let's not waste another moment. The game is already underway, and the cold of winter is deepening by the hour. Preparations must be made.

BUT, BEFORE WE START, LET'S STATE THE FACTS AND DISPEL THE MYTHS

Back in late 2021, when the markets were raging with cash-drunk consumers, investors, and economists, I called my shot and made an unpopular forecast - recession, no worse, *depression*, would rock modern life as we know it within 24-36 months.

Despite all of the economists and "experts" at the time saying that the economy was healthy and there was a near zero risk of recession anytime soon, I, along with a *very* small group of others, was sure of it.

The housing market was going *absolutely* insane with bidding wars for homes listed at double a home's value. The labor market was upside down with 2-3 open jobs per person, forcing employers to pay ~160% what a person was worth… just to fill their most critical gaps and keep the doors open. The stock market was accelerating at a pace never before seen with higher-than-ever valuations; all fueled by *imaginary* money created by governments and crypto entrepreneurs around the world.

And these were just the top-level issues. Don't even get me started on how people were slacking off and producing less (quiet quitting), or how businesses were selling goods and services that they _had no hope of actually delivering_ for at least 12-24 months (supply chain and labor backlog), or how prices of everything were starting to reach record year-over-year gains (inflation).

At the time, the vast majority of people thought that these were all good things. In their minds, it was a post pandemic boom that would never end. Consequences weren't even a consideration.

But I, along with that *very* small percentage of the population I mentioned earlier, was convinced with every morsel of my being that a *deep* economic winter was coming. You might have been in the same boat with me; one of the few.

Now, at the time of this writing, and less than a year later, the "cold" is beginning to set into the economy. Inflation is flat-out out of control. Revenue targets at businesses across industries are being missed, by a lot. Central banks are walking back their "easy money" policies and jacking up interest rates. Workers are beginning to be laid off en-masse. Small business owners are racking up debts as they try stay afloat. Consumers are struggling to pay their bills. And the bad news just keeps on coming.

All in all, forecasts for the future are not pretty… and <u>I'm no longer in the minority of those who believe that dark times are ahead</u>.

But that's all beside the point here. You didn't pick up this book so that you could hear a bunch of doom and gloom about all the things that you now know to be true. You picked it up so that you might learn about what you need to do *right now* in order to prepare yourself and your business to survive the coming winter, and even come out of it in better shape than when you entered.

So, to back things up to what I began a year ago when I was still in the minority of economic calamity believers…

To prepare for the tough times I foresaw, I did something that caused most of my friends and family to think I had lost my mind. I sold *every* asset I owned that I didn't, or couldn't, control the outcome of. In a nutshell, that means that I offloaded every stock I owned, I sold every business that I didn't think I could focus intently on during tough times, and fired every customer that I didn't see as my "best" (yes, customers are an asset that, in a way, you own).

I then used the extra bandwidth I had made for myself to research recessions, depressions, and economic "blips" in an attempt to find the time-tested strategies that businesses used to survive, and more importantly, grow during tough times.

Let's be frank, before my research, I was **not** an expert in recessions, depressions, or any other kind of down economic cycle. I was just a regular entrepreneur managing a handful of decently successful businesses. I had a coffee business, a marketing and sales consultancy, a home services company, a couple of books, and a few contract sales engagements to my name.

I was just your average entrepreneur.

By no means was I qualified to write a book about how to survive and thrive during tough economies. If asked on the spot, I would not be able to answer the question:

"How Can A Business Prepare For A Recession?"

But now I can. Why? Because every situation has happened before. The down economy that we are headed into is not new to history. Sure, there are some technological and political factors that are more unique today than in past economic cycles, but the principles all remain the same. Humans are still taking cash out of their bank account to pay for goods and services. The psychology of how they do that, and what makes them choose one option over the other, has not changed. Biology and psychology remain a constant.

The honest fact here is that people will behave in the way they always have. For all of the modern advancement we have today, the best – and only – indicator for what will happen and how to best handle this recession is to research the down cycles of the past.

So, that's what I did.

I searched through the lessons of old – through the stories about companies and what they did, as well through the accounts of verifiable business experts of their time – for the nuggets of wisdom that would help in the times ahead.

The information that I pulled from the tomes of history is quite literally gold, and those who heed the suggestions made in this book will be the prospector; efficiently pulling nuggets out while others around them swirl empty pans.

If being fully honest, though…

This Book Is Not The Only Source Of This Information.

In no way shape or form am I so arrogant to sit here behind my keyboard and tell you that the learnings and lessons contained within this book are some sort of "secret". They are not. This information can be readily obtained by anyone, at any time… _**if**_ that person is willing to put in the research and work (while applying a fair bit of deductive reasoning).

If you so wish, you can do just as I did and spend 6+ months digging through the tomes of time trying to find the nuggets buried within. Or you could take the old-fashioned route of trial-and-erroring your way through hypotheses in order to find the solutions for yourself; if you're willing to test, fail, and iterate until you find the right path, of course.

At the end of the day, there are many options in front of you for how to obtain the information contained within this book. It'll be up to you to decide what works best for you - a verifiable shortcut printed on a couple hundred pages (this book)… or the hard way of doing it yourself.

If you so choose, this book can shortcut your path to recession growth while _illuminating_ a clearer path than what you otherwise might find.

The Time Is Near

At the time of this writing in fall 2022, the global economy is creaking, cracking, and getting ready to take on water. The "unsinkable" Titanic economy that everyone has been riding for decades has hit the iceberg of its fate.

Markets are down over 25% from their all-time highs, governments and central banks around the world are freaking out about uncontrollable inflation, and major "economic bedrock" companies – the kind that hold up the entire global economy – are reporting hefty revenue misses… and are substantially down trending their forecasts as a result.

Oh, and the heads of major banks, like Jamie Dimon of JP Morgan, and billionaires like Elon Musk (Tesla), Sundar Pichai (Google), and Jeff Bezos (Amazon), are all sounding the alarm. "It's time to batten down the hatches", according to Bezos.

INTRODUCTION

They wouldn't be saying these things if something insurmountably difficult weren't ahead of us. They see a storm unlike anything the world has ever seen coming our way.

The outlook is not rosy.

The good news, though, is that we may still have some time before things start to get hairy. I'd wager 6-9 months at this point; putting us at May, June, or July 2023 when we begin to see the worst of it beginning to truly set in.

Just enough time to prepare.

RECESSION PROOF

The Curse Of Modern Business & Why It Is The Key To Growth In Tough Times.

PREFACE

In today's world, the life of an average business owner is much different than it was 30 years ago (when the last dual recession and rampant inflation hit). Back then, the world was much simpler.

Consumers went to their local store or provider – often the only one of its kind in their area – to get what they needed. Cash was exchanged for goods and services, and if they ended up not liking what they had purchased they took it up with the owner directly.

Simple as simple could be.

So, when inflation and a recession hit at the same time back in the 70s/80s, solutions were much easier to find and implement. Sure, there was some widespread pain, but, for the most of it, small business owners still ruled the roost in the broader economy and were able to recover quickly. The simplicity of business played in their favor.

Compare that to today, and business owners face a _much_ different landscape.

Today, if I decided that I wanted to go buy, say, dog food, I could swing around the corner to my local pet food store to look for the brand and flavor that my dog likes. If the store doesn't have it, or if I don't like their price, no worries. I can always check Amazon and have it delivered next day. And, if for some strange reason I can't find it on Amazon then I'll surely be able to find it at Petco, Chewy.com, or a whole host of other places that carry it in stock and sell it at a price that I like.

The options available to me, and all consumers, are nearly endless. Anyone, anywhere, at any time of day can buy pretty much anything that they could want. There are very few restrictions to buying, so people buy freely.

At first glance, this may seem to be a good thing for businesses. Customers can buy anything they want seamlessly and without friction. By definition, that should describe the golden era of business… and not be a "problem" defined as an opening idea in a book about saving your business in a recession.

But a problem it is, and here's why – **excessive choice.**

With the ability to buy almost anything at any time from almost anywhere (excessive choice) comes a nasty little thing that business owners should despise with all of their being, commoditization.

For those not 100% familiar with the term, commoditization is the market force that drives consumers to price shop (and get away with it without repercussion). Said a different way, it's the thing that causes companies in the same industry to compete on price in a bid to win customers. The result is most often plummeting prices and razor thin margins (if not negative margins).

These are tough conditions for small business owners to operate in for sure.

Nothing in this world should be more infuriating to a business owner than commoditization. Not staffing headaches. Not returns and customer disputes. And certainly not the cost of marketing. **Commoditization is the kryptonite sucking the life force out of you and your business.**

That's because commoditization erodes margins... and eroding margins force businesses to sell in mass quantity. Selling in mass quantity often leads itself to selling at lower quality. It's a downward spiral in nearly every regard.

During good economies, while annoying, commoditization can often be ignored by businesses. _It probably shouldn't be ignored_, but it can be... and most often is. That's because _quantity_ of sales is relatively easy to come by in good economies. Consumers are buying freely, after all.

But There's A Catch...

During tough economies, commoditization is often the single biggest reason for, and cause of, business failure and bankruptcy. As consumers tighten their purse strings and buy more selectively, sales volume shrinks.

At first when this happens, businesses do the smart thing and try to maintain their margins despite declining sales. They'll hold this position for a while until the pressure from decreasing sales volumes creates some **real** discomfort in the business. Then, a bunch of really smart people will gather in groups and sit in meeting rooms trying to strategize on ways that they can improve sales without price reductions. Many great ideas come out of these sessions, but at the end of the day, month, and quarter, their sales volume will come up short.

It is at this point when the excuses and explanations start to come on fast. Smart people try to rationalize their failures. Desperation begins to set in.

This is when the knee jerk reaction happens. Businesses concede to market pressures and lower their prices, rates, and retainers - or deliver more for the same price (which is essentially a price reduction) – all in a bid to maintain the *quantity* of sales they need.

As competitors see each other racing to maintain sales volumes, **_Deflation_** begins to set in. The downward spiral begins, and businesses begin to fail.

Believe it or not, I believe this is a good thing. Not just a good thing, actually, but a GREAT thing… **_but only for the businesses that are prepared for it._**

More on that later.

At the time of this writing, it is earnings season, and we are right at the tip of *formally* going into a recession. Companies are at stage 1 of the downward spiral described above. They've just suffered through their first few quarters of missed revenue targets and are sitting in meeting rooms strategizing on solutions.

Very few of them will "get" it. They'll have all these great and wonderful ideas about how they'll survive and thrive, but they'll miss the mark. They **_WILL_** go through the cycle described above and fall into the spiral.

Meanwhile, the people who have read this book and implemented its teachings will thrive. They'll enjoy groundbreaking profit margins and undeterred growth as they <u>snag all of their competitor's **best**</u> customers; leaving their competitor to deal with the "worst" customers that remain (the bargain shoppers, complainers, etc.).

And just like that, commoditization will become a good thing because…

It Will Force Your Competitors Out Of Business While You Position For Profits.

Recessions, and the price deflation that typically come with them, are a good thing *for smart business owners and leaders* who prepare well for tough times just as much as they do for good times. Most business owners don't do this. Instead, they focus on growth during good times and then moan and begroan as soon as good times end.

They play the game of business as if the rules haven't changed, and then complain about how they are "unfairly" getting pushed around and passed over in the market. Grumble as they do, it doesn't change the fact that, indeed, the rules have changed and what worked before is not likely to work now.

That's why you're going to change your business to align with the new rules – rules that apply only to you, as the sole competitor in a new game. Why? Because the chances are that if you're reading this book then you run a *small to mid-sized* business. You're not a huge company and don't have oodles of capital backing you. You're "disadvantaged"… but only in the sense of the old rules.

Your competitors are likely to be better funded, have entire teams of very smart people, have better brand presence, and have better distribution channels. **They would, and will, crush you if you play the same game as them.**

That's why you're going to create your own game. One where you manufacture market demand for *your* products and services without allowing for customers to compare you to anyone else.

You're going to create your very own game of Monopoly. And, if played correctly, you're going to command your market. Customers will jump over hurdles to do business with you, other businesses will seek to collaborate with you, and employees will come to you ready to work for less than market rates.

PREFACE

Sound too good to be true? Read on.

RECESSION PROOF

The Indicators That Determine If Your Business Will Survive A Down Economy.

RECESSION PROOF

Before we dive into how you can leverage commoditization as a growth driver in your business…

What If I Told You That You Could <u>Know</u> With Relative Certainty That Your Business Will Survive and Grow Through *Any* Economic Down Cycle?

Well, you can.

One of the clearest themes across all of history is that nearly every business that gained ground during recessions shared a set of indicators that preceded the strategies and tactics that they employed.

Note the word **"*preceded*"** here. These indicators weren't things present in their strategies and tactics but were things that informed and influenced what they did in their business and how they did it. The indicators *led* their business. They were choices made by business leaders that embedded a certain philosophy and ideal throughout their organization.

If the business had these ideals, their chances of success during tough times exponentially increased. The same will be true throughout this recession, and all others after it. They are evergreen ideals often overlooked during good economies, but critical during bad ones.

Ready to hear what they are?

THE THREE OBSESSIONS

The indicators for knowing if your business will survive and thrive through this, and any, down economic cycle are a set of three *obsessions*. If you have them, your business will be substantially more likely to coast through the market turbulence with relative ease. If you don't have them, your business simply might not make it through the storm.

So, if you take away nothing else from this book, take this: **these three obsessions will be the most important aspect of your success in the coming months and years**. They alone will be the reason for all that you achieve or don't achieve.

These obsessions are:

i.   An obsession with the customer and their experience with your business.

ii. An obsession with serving a growing number of customers.

iii. An obsession with continually improving results.

Everything else that we cover in this book will be a subset of these obsessions. Every strategy that we cover, every tactic that we outline, every tool that we recommend, every case study that we review, everything, will all fall under one of these three obsessions.

Naturally, as you read through this book you will want to skip through parts of it in order to get to the "meaty" stuff - the stuff that you feel you need in your business right now. For most, this means that they will jump straight to the section where we cover how to get more customers (obsession #2).

While you certainly *can* do this, it is not advised to do so. Yes, the first section of this book - customer obsession - may have some parts that feel redundant if you've been in business a while... but that doesn't mean that you shouldn't revisit the key points in the section and solidify that you have them down, because you probably don't.

So much of business is **fundamentals**, and at the core of these obsessions... are fundamentals. So, let's review.

OBSESSION 1 - An Obsession With Your Customer And Their Experience With Your Business

Most good business owners know that the #1 rule in business is that the customer comes first. That's not to say that all transactions lean in their favor or that they must always be right. Good god, no. It simply means that customers should get at least what they paid for.

A good customer experience, at its bare minimum, <u>is an expectation met</u>; with the exchange of money for value being fair. This is the foundation of all business.

The thing is, in good economies, it can be easy for some business owners to become a bit lax in various areas of their business. Heck, they can even break this rule willfully, and repeatedly, yet still do just fine. The sheer number of people looking for solutions drastically outnumbers the providers, and certain things can be overlooked.

It never ceases to surprise me how many businesses break this first rule of business. Their business is all about *them*; their great product or service, their amazing features, their company's phenomenal growth, their profitability, their lofty goals, their bank account… their ego. <u>For many companies, the customer is an afterthought</u>. Customers are a mere part of the equation that they would happily remove or do away with if it weren't the fact that they are where the money comes from.

Said in other words, most businesses are narcissists. Focused almost exclusively on themselves.

Take for example all the home contractors who took their customer's money for "a week's long project" and then dilly-dallied for 6 months before they completed the job… and completed it with piss-poor quality, I might add. The customer could complain, report them to the Better Business Bureau, or even sue all they wanted. The contractors didn't care much about delivering a fair exchange of money for value (if they cared at all). They got their money, and that's all that mattered to them. "To hell with the customer", is the message they sent into the market.

Or, another example, all the restaurants, medical offices, and other types of businesses that decided one day that they would no longer answer their phones for new bookings, respond to customer service requests, or deliver quality work or products because it was "too much of a hassle to do so". They opted to become selfish instead of providing service to their customers and prospects, focusing almost exclusively on their own needs and wellbeing.

In these examples, and in a hundred more that I could give you, businesses were able to get away with providing the minimum for their customers. Times were good, customers were plenty, and for every person who said "I'll never use them again" there were 10 more lined up practically begging for their products and services. Not because of the quality they offered, but because there was simply *nobody* else to turn to.

It's easy to do business in that kind of economy. It takes very little effort for an imbecile with a sign to run profitably. **_But_** the moment that the economy starts to turn, <u>as it is now</u>, those businesses that *didn't* have a customer obsession will be the first to die.

The slowed economic activity will mean fewer customers lining up to work with them. And fewer customers lining up means that quality, service, and customer experience matters a whole heck of a lot. In a down economy, **_customer choice_ becomes the scythe of the economic grim reaper** and customer experience becomes the measure by which choices are judged.

A poor customer experience will no longer be tolerated by the market. Not only that, as economic activity dwindles, even a *normal* customer experience won't be enough. Competition for customers will be tight.

That's why…

In Times Ahead, The Business That Can Provide The Best Customer Experience, Profitably, Will Thrive.

Read that again, because it's important.

The business that can provide the best customer experience, while remaining profitable, will outlast all others as they <u>absorb the best customers in their market</u>. That's because as every other business around them crumbles, becomes desperate, and suffocates themselves in the race to the bottom of price, the business that deliver the best experience will be able to maintain higher prices, higher margins, lower customer churn, and more new customer referrals.

Customer experience will be the moat that they build around their business, protecting them from the economically fueled war taking place around them.

That brings me to a question:

> # "How Confident Are You That You Provide <u>The Best</u> Customer Experience In Your Market?"

If you're anything like I was when I first learned about the customer obsession principle then you might be having an "oh, shit…" moment right now as you read this.

You're delivering value to your clients… but nothing extraordinary, right?

It's okay, most entrepreneurs and business owners are in the same spot. The good news… most of them will be out of business shortly, and you'll have your act together, obsessed with your customer and their experience, delivering extraordinary value to them.

We'll cover *how* you'll do that momentarily. In the meantime…

OBSESSION 2 - An Obsession With Serving A *Growing* Number Of Customers

To quote the legendary marketing and business mind, Dan Kennedy, "without a sufficient and steady stream of people with whom you can exchange value for money, nothing else about your business matters. Not your most excellent website. Not your high visibility location. Not your credentials, degrees, certifications, education, etc. Not your hard-working "nose-to-the-grindstone" work ethic." Not even your exceptional customer experience.

Being the best at what you do is great and all, but it means absolutely nothing if you don't have a steady stream of customers. This is evermore true during recessions when customers are more scarce.

If the source of your cash flow (customers) is drying up then it won't matter that you went to Harvard, just opened a shiny new location with all the bells and whistles, or just had your website prettied up by a professional web designer. There is no "business" that all of these things represent without customers flowing through your door with cash in hand.

Most business owners are not willing to accept this reality.

In concept, they "get it" but they can't seem to let go of the paradigm embedded in their mind by years of societal conditioning that "better" should be enough. That better credentials… better experience…better work ethic… better quality… and all the other "betters" used throughout history *SHOULD* automatically equate to customers knocking at their door with cash in hand. Surely, these things do matter. But they only matter when there are customers to serve. Without customers, everything that a business has and has put together are just wall decorations and good intentions. Meaningless memorabilia.

It's not until a business owner comes to the realization – with full "aha" moment – that their business *IS* their customer base and not their products and/or services that they begin to grasp the concept that…

You Have No Business Without A Steady Stream Of Customers

Just like how in Monopoly you have no revenue without little plastic houses on the board and other players passing through, in real life you have no business without customers flowing through your doors. Nothing matters without customers, because customers are the only thing that makes your business… a business.

That leads us to what is probably the most important question in this book:

How Do You Attract A Steady Stream Of Customers During A Recession?

Before I answer this question, let's first preface the situation in which the problem exists.

During recessions, the causal factor of decreased economic activity is a national (or global) consumer base that for real or imagined reasons is spending less money. This might be because they lost their jobs… or because inflation has caused them to tighten purse strings… or because they simply have a fear that rainy days are coming.

It might even be a combination of all three of the above (a particularly dire situation, and one that we're in now).

As consumers and businesses spend less, the pool of buyers for any given product or service shrinks and it becomes increasingly difficult for businesses to attract enough customers to support expenditures and remain profitable. Said another way, marketing to a *shrinking* customer pool becomes more expensive under the traditional model of marketing. For many, it becomes too expensive.

The key words to focus in on above are ***traditional marketing***. You know, all those signs and billboards on the side of the road, broadly targeted mailers in the mailbox, premium physical locations, social media posts and ads sent into oblivion, and all the rest of the noise made in an effort to <u>randomly</u> capture the attention of people who <u>potentially</u> might have interest in a product or service.

Unfortunately, this is most marketing today; a bunch of poorly put together messages crafted by people who think that marketing is a verb – an *action* repeated enough times for the message to, *eventually*, capture the attention of a random interested party who, maybe, just maybe, might buy.

Hint, marketing, at least good marketing, ***is not a verb***.

While marketing as a verb described above might work during times of plenty, it is much less likely to work in times of scarcity when every business under the sun ratchets up the same "blah" marketing that they did during the good ol' days of a booming economy. The marketplace quickly gets noisy, and customers, even more quickly, tune it out.

What worked before no longer works. Massive marketing action quickly becomes a waste of time. A new strategy is needed in order to keep a steady flow of customers coming to you with cash in hand.

Enter marketing <u>as a noun</u> – a fixed asset that can be described as a "thing", not an activity.

But, recognizing that this will be confusing if you've never heard it before, allow me to explain…

"Marketing, Done Correctly, Is Not Something That You Do… But Something That You OWN."

What this means is that your marketing should be like real estate, a fixed structure that is not often changed, modified, or added to. When maintained, it provides for all of your basic needs, and more. You own it.

PREFACE

I get it, though. It still doesn't make sense…

To offer an example, in my own marketing for my main business (sales copywriting & consulting) I don't have a Facebook page, Instagram account, YouTube channel, networking group, or really anything else that most businesses consider to be their "marketing". To me, these things are all marketing as a verb. They're all things that I have to "do" and keep up with, often, if I want any value out of them at all. They take up a ton of time and, in reality, offer only marginal results, at best. These are the epitome of marketing as a verb.

Instead, I use a two-page printed sales letter, mailed in an envelope with stamp that I lick, sent to _very_ targeted business owners who I _know_ are buyers of services like mine. The letter that I use is a template (don't tell) but reads as though I have done tremendous research on their company. It directs them to a sales page where I have a low-resistance offer that is <u>difficult for them to refuse</u>; complete with a deadline for action, or they lose out.

If they don't bite and buy on the first letter, I send them a few more… all driving to the deadline that helps motivate action.

That's it. That right there is the main driver of my business. A single, very simple, **asset** of targeted sales letter + sales page + follow up letters. That asset delivers the work that I need and want. If I want to scale it up or diversify my lead sources, I can either send more letters or modify the letter for other media (e.g. running ads or content in other media channels where I _know_ my customers frequent and give their attention).

I don't need to spend/waste a bunch of time posting to social media, attending networking groups, or all that other junk. I have an asset that I can employ that is more than capable of driving my business forward, in good economies and bad.

You should too, but before we get to that…

OBSESSION 3 - An Obsession With Continually Improving Results

The third and final obsession that will indicate your business' success in a tough economy is the obsession with continually improving your results, in every aspect of your business. From your marketing to your staffing, to your operations, to your hiring, contracting, and everything in between.

Every activity performed in, for, or on your business has a _cost_ and an _outcome_. Because of this, every activity can be tracked, analyzed, and improved so that you as a business leader can understand what moves the needle the furthest in the most cost-effective manner. Big companies do this exceptionally well.

Take Amazon for example. If you've ever read up on Amazon's obsession with continually improving results, or have ever worked there and seen it firsthand, you will see how they track _everything_ (quite literally). Every step, every package moved, every product lost or misplaced, every second it takes for a package to go from ordered, to boxed, to shipped and delivered. Not just that, every search, click, scroll, add to cart, remove from cart, and other activity on their site, app, and video streaming app is tracked and measured (along with almost everything else you can think of).

Everything is tracked, analyzed, and improved upon so that they can deliver the best customer experience at the lowest cost while maintaining the best possible margins. It's smart business if you ask me.

Sadly, though, very few small business owners have this level of obsession with continually improving results. They most certainly _like_ results and want to see more of them… but they aren't overly obsessed with tracking and continuously improving the metrics that drive those results across the business.

This lack of metrics obsession means that most small business owners know very little about what drives results in their business. They just go about their days doing _stuff_; whatever they so happen to think is the best use of their time on any given day.

PREFACE

So, when the economy starts to get shaky, their anxiety level tends to skyrocket. They've been doing "stuff" for so long, without *knowing* if it's actually the right thing to be doing, that they find themselves trying a bunch of "stuff" and hoping that something works. It's the proverbial story about throwing garbage against the wall to see what sticks, and it's horribly inefficient. It wastes time and money for the business owner… at a time when time and money are absolutely critical.

The good news here is that it's not hard to start obsessing over the metrics in your business. Often times, it can start with tracking the activities you are doing for customer experience (obsession #1) and acquiring new customers (obsession #2). For example, you can begin tracking:

- If a welcome package sent to customers after their first order has a meaningful impact on customer satisfaction, retention, purchase frequency, lifetime value, etc.
- If sending existing customers a print newsletter monthly results in an increase in transaction volume and value (hint: it should).
- If your sales letter or advertisement is attracting your ideal customers – the ones you want to have frequenting your business – at a rate that enables you to profitably bring in new customers.
- If your targeting is putting your offer in front of the right people so that you see optimized lead conversion.

As you begin to establish systems and processes for tracking metrics, you can add additional KPI (key performance indicators) to the mix so that you can further optimize your business. The possibilities for *what* you might track are nearly endless, though, and that can be a problem.

Just because you can track something, doesn't mean that you should. The fact of the matter is that you *don't* need to track an endless number of metrics in order to be obsessed with continually improving your results. That would simply be too chaotic for most small businesses.

Instead, all you need to track are your core few KPI – the indicators specific to your business that tell you if you're headed in the right direction or not. Then when you see that a core KPI metric is not performing at a level that you'd like to see, you can dive into the sub-metrics within that area so that you can **objectively** determine root causes and implement intelligent mitigations and/or improvements.

All that said, that's about as deep as we'll go into the obsession with continually improving results here in this book, because, well, this topic simply has too many variables to coherently organize on a few hundred pages. So, we'll focus in on the first two obsessions and leave this third one just to what we've covered so far.

A Little Structure, For Sanity & Action

It is as at this point in the book that we'll transition from the generics of what the problem is (an impending recession that you may or may not be prepared for) and what the potential solutions are at a high level… to the specific strategies and tactics that you can employ to prepare your business and make it more resilient to the pressures of a down economy.

To do that in an efficient and effective manner, the rest of this book will (mostly) follow a defined structure that should make it easy to follow along and even easier to refer back to when it comes time to implement.

If you're anything like me, then you've read dozens of books in your lifetime that each got you really excited about an idea that you were **sure** to action on. The idea consumed your consciousness for about a week… and then disappeared into the ether… never to be actioned on in a meaningful way.

That can't happen with this book. The stakes are too high with the current economic climate. So, from here forward, all chapters will be broken down into three parts:

1. An overarching concept
2. The strategy defining that concept
3. The tactics that will allow you to make progress on the strategy (and overarching concept as a whole).

PREFACE

While this structure will make the book seem a bit choppier than many other books you have read, it will also make it easier for you to digest the concepts being shared so that you can read fast and implement faster. Literary excellence is not the goal here, actionable insights are. The intent is to make a point, communicate a direction, and move on quickly so that you can – in as short a time as possible – implement.

As such, <u>a bias for action is necessary</u>.

There is no need to read this book if you don't intend to act quickly on what you learn. So, don't read and then ponder about what you are going to do for weeks on end. Read a chapter, or even just a few tactics at a time, critically think about how you might implement in your business, and then act.

It doesn't need to be any more complicated than that.

RECESSION PROOF

PART 1

An Obsession With Your Customer & Their Experience With Your Business

RECESSION PROOF

As mentioned in the last chapter, being the company that provides the best customer experience in your market has tremendous value. While other businesses suffer the fates doled out to them as a result of customer choice and commoditization, the business that customers *prefer* to patronize will operate as if they were still in a booming economy.

The question you likely have at this point is…

"How Do You Become The Business That Customers Prefer To Patronize?"

It's a great question and is one that has many different components that can be added like legos in order to create a rock solid business. Customer satisfaction, excitement, loyalty, preference, referrals, and unwavering support can all be built using the various components that we'll cover here in Part 1 of this book.

But before we get to all of that…

THE CONCEPT

In concept, customer obsession is fairly straightforward – do what you can in order to make your customers happy.

Simple, right?

In reality, the keys to true customer satisfaction – to the point where they are raving fans – is more nuanced than most realize. It's not as simple as delivering more for them and doing so with a helpful smile. That might have worked 30 years ago when the marketplace was simpler and less competitive than it is now, but in today's world the "overdeliver and be friendly" strategy will only get you so far.

Today, if you want to make your business more resilient to recessionary forces then you will need to create a business where your customers:

1. Are <u>unwilling</u> to give your competitors a chance because they are _emotionally invested_ in your business.
2. Willingly <u>pay you higher prices</u> because they believe that they get more value through you.
3. Have a compelling desire to <u>tell others about your business</u>.

Just imagine what you might achieve if your customers exhibited these 3 traits. You'd have more repeat sales and inbound customer referrals than you'd know what to do with, and all at higher margins. Under these conditions, your business would become unbreakable. You yourself would be the _invincible_ entrepreneur of the ~~year~~ decade.

Here's the thing, though: this isn't just some pipe dream that can never happen for you. Having customers who exhibit these three traits is more common than you might think, and more achievable than you might realize. To rattle off a few companies that I myself am a customer exhibiting these traits for: Clickfunnels, Magnetic Marketing/GKIC, Under Armour, Axiom, and range of others.

Outside of Under Armour, all of these companies are small to mid-sized companies that have "herded" me into their world, given me an exceptional experience, and made me a raving fan. And, if they can do it, then so can you... **_IF_** you have a Customer Obsession within your business.

That's because the entire concept of Customer Obsession is driven by the three traits we covered above. That's it. Once you've achieved a state where your customers...

1. Have an objection to buying from and supporting anyone but you,
2. Willingly spend more money with you, and
3. Go out of their way to tell others about you

PART 1 – CUSTOMER OBSESSION

…then you know that you have established a Customer Obsessed business that will be resilient to any economic downtrend.

To paraphrase the leader of a business who achieved all 3 of these customer obsessed outcomes, Steve Jobs of Apple, if you are looking to create a business with a rock-solid foundation and level of resiliency to weather any economic storm, **you need to start at the customer experience and then work backwards from there**. Strangely, or maybe not so strangely, around the same time, in the late 90's, Jeff Bezos of Amazon embedded this same philosophy as a core tenet of his business. It led both of their businesses to rapid growth and resiliency through good economies and bad.

Long ago, when I was just starting my first businesses, I did the *exact opposite* of this. I would spend hours upon hours dreaming up ideas for my new business; how it would operate, how I'd get customers, how much money I would make, and all the rest. I was *obsessed* with my business. I fell in love with all the sales and marketing I would do, with the layout of the building that I'd build, and with the life that it would all afford me. In my dreams, my business was perfect.

I thought I was SO smart for dreaming it up.

But, in all of my scheming and dreaming, do you know what I *wasn't* obsessed with? What I didn't give much consideration to?

My customer.

In all of my business planning the *ONE* person who would actually give me money was but a mere afterthought. A part of the business equation that I didn't value enough to plan around.

I didn't give much thought to what my customer's experience would be like with my new business because I never realized how much they mattered (rookie move). I figured that what I would create would be so amazing that they would have no choice but to become customers for life the moment that they learned of my business.

Well. shortly after launching my new business, reality set in. I quickly learned that…

People Like Self-Centered Businesses About As Much As They Like Self-Centered People.
(They Don't)

That's a hard truth for many business owners to come to terms with. It certainly was for me.

I've since cleaned up my ways... but am never surprised by the sheer number of businesses who haven't. Still obsessed with their own businesses and levels of success, entrepreneurs today *too often* overlook the most important part of their business – the ONLY thing that actually makes them a business and not a hobby – their customers.

Just take a look at businesses all around you. The vast majority of them, especially since the pandemic, operate and exist around <u>what is convenient for them</u>. For example, cable and internet companies hand customers 9-10 hour time windows for when their technician will come out. Then, if you don't answer the technician's call at the precise moment that they pull up to your house then they will cancel your appointment and reschedule you. They don't care one iota about their customer's experience.

On a similar note, restaurants have limited or cut their menus, hours of operation, and willingness to answer their phones, while also slashing the customer service expectations of their staff. Going out to eat at many restaurants today is now as much a bad experience as it is an enjoyable one.

I could go on, but the bigger question is this: **What will happen to all of these businesses when the recession sets in and customers adopt more spendthrift ways?**

I'll tell you. Either they will switch gears and work at becoming a whole heck of a lot more customer obsessed... or they will throw up their hands in frustration and go out of business. Mark my words, those will be their only two options.

Doom and gloom aside, let's bring things back to what we really need to cover here – creating a business that is so customer obsessed that customers begin to exhibit the 3 traits.

Naturally, creating a business where your customers resist patronizing anyone but you, knowingly and willingly pay you higher prices, and provide unsolicited referrals is not as simple as just overdelivering and being helpful in your business. You have to be very intentional about creating an experience for your customers that fosters the development of these traits within them. This will take months, sometimes years, but that shouldn't deter you from the path.

So, let's get walking…

RECESSION PROOF

The Customer That "Knows" The Owner

RECESSION PROOF

THE STRATEGY

Have you ever noticed how companies – both large and small – that have an owner who is present, visible, and likable tend to dominate a market? You know, those companies where you _feel_ like you "know" the owner (even if you really don't and you just know _of_ them).

If you haven't noticed these companies before then you should begin taking note. Amazon would not be what it is without Jeff Bezos being so visible. Tesla, the same with Elon Musk. Microsoft the same with Bill Gates. Berkshire Hathaway, the same with Warren Buffett. The list goes on and on.

But it's not just the giant mega companies with billionaire leaders where this is the case. In nearly every local market there is:

- An automobile dealer who _everyone_ in that locale "knows", and they are typically the most well-known and "best" dealer in the area.
- A restaurant or two led by owners that _everyone_ seems to know, and they are often the "best" restaurants in town with hard-to-get reservations (even in down economies).
- A dentist, chiropractor, and even fitness trainer who _everyone_ has heard about and feels as though they know them.
- A boutique or beauty shop with an owner known as the "best" in the area because of the reputation of the owner. And _everyone_ seems to know who the owner is.

Starting to see a trend here? The "best" companies in every local, national, and international market have an owner who is front and center; promoting _themselves_ as synonymous with the business. It's not about all of their fancy schmancy stuff, superior amazing products and services, or their "top notch" team (at all). It's about the owner, every time. Everything else communicated about the business is just an offshoot of the owner's public personality and persona. **The star of the show is, hands down, the owner**.

These owners have positioned themselves as the people who you feel like you know, like, and trust. As such, they feel like a friend of sorts that people in their market want to support and be associated with.

<u>That's the goal here for you</u> – to become a figure within your market who is well known, liked, and supported because your customers view you as someone that they "know", like, and trust... like a friend. This is one of the first steps for becoming customer obsessed (even though it might not seem like it at first).

THE TACTICS:

A Personality To Love, A Person To Trust

Almost nobody wants to be friends with a monotone robot who never has an opinion, or does anything fun, or takes a stand for what they believe in. Yet, most business owners behave this way; monotone robots who hide - or outright lack - any personality.

Hardly anybody knows that they own their business. Fewer would pay attention if they were told about the owner. "Oh, that's great!", might be a common response received from a patron who learns of the ownership.

That's a waste.

People in your industry and market _need_ to know who you are. They need to know what you do. They need to know what you're up to. They need to <u>want to be a part of it</u>.

- If you're a restaurant owner, they need to want to go to "Tony's restaurant".
- If you're a consultant, they need to think to themselves "I need Tasha's help".
- If you're an author, they need to be eagerly awaiting "Jim's next book".

You get the point here. Your customers need to know you, what you do, and what you're up to (including things that are upcoming). Oh, and they need to feel as though they like you.

To make this happen, you need to get out of your shell and become the personality that they know, like, trust, and want to be around. That means that you need to have, or create, a strong personality; a personality that your ideal customer would want to be friends with. Big, but not boastful. Energetic, but not over the top. Bold, but not overstepping.

Without this personality, your customers will never know, or care, about who you are. That's why you need to get yourself one, quickly.

There are entire books on this topic, but none better than Expert Secrets by Russell Brunson. Instead of myself pretending to be the authority on the topic, I'll simply direct you to his book at the QR code below (where he gives it to you for FREE). Go ahead and scan it if you'd like to learn how to create a personality that your customers want to follow:

"I See You Everywhere" Effect

What's the point of having a personality if nobody ever gets a chance to see it? If you want to enjoy the benefits of your customers knowing you, liking you, and trusting you then you are going to need to put yourself out there. The more places, the better.

- Your ads should have a picture of you front and center, or otherwise feature you in the creative.
- Every new customer should get to meet you (even if only through a virtual or email introduction of who you are).
- Your radio spots should feature you.
- The political candidates that you support should be required to have a picture of you with a statement of "[your name] supports [candidate] for office".

Okay, the last one might be a bit much for most businesses, but you get the point. You – or another co-owner if you have one – need to become the face of your business. That is, unless you're like State Farm Insurance and can afford to pay a brand representative on a multi-year retainer to be the face for you… but we're going to assume that you're not like State Farm.

That means that it's on you as the owner of your business to step up and be the person, the personality, that everyone attributes with your business. Everywhere that you can possibly put your face and name that your customers might see and pay attention to, you should.

When people begin to see you and your personality, they will associate your business with you. As they do, your business will reap the benefits of people beginning to feel as though "they know the owner".

A Little Polarity Never Hurts

Like in politics, many business owners try to walk a fine line on issues of the day so as to steer clear of finding themselves in hot water. They view taking a stance one way or the other as being high risk for the business… with very little potential reward, if any.

Nothing could be further from the truth.

People with personality have opinions, beliefs, and even enemies. They don't hold these back. Instead, they champion them. They take a stance, make a statement, and hold their ground.

Their customers – the ones who *think* like them – gravitate in their direction as a result, drawn to their polarity.

Just look at every public personality that you follow and/or pay attention to. They have strong opinions and beliefs, don't they? Chances are, they're willing to hold their ground on issues that matter to them, and to make and have enemies of those who sit on the opposite side of their beliefs. That's why you like them. They say and do the things that you agree with, and as a result you give them your attention and support.

You must do the same.

You have to say and do the things that your ideal customers agree with, even if that means you push away other customers who might disagree with you. It's okay to not be for everyone, because by not being for everyone you become *more* for the right type of person, the type of person that you most want to serve in your business.

This is the foundation for having die-hard customers – the kind who will support you through thick and thin, good and bad. The kind that you're going to need when times get tough.

But here's the thing, you have to make sure that your personality and the polarizing topics that you choose to publicly take a stance are:

1. Aligned to the core beliefs of the customers that you most want to serve in your business (your ideal customers).
2. Are relevant to your business, or can be made relevant.
3. Supported by a market that has enough of your ideal customers within it.

Too often, I see business owners jumping into the wrong polarizing topics that don't meet the criteria above. They push an agenda that alienates the core beliefs of their best customers, or they take a stance on a topic that they can't tie back to their business in any way, or they promote an ideology that isn't supported by enough customers in their market. These are all bad scenarios that business owners should, and can, avoid by making sure that the polarizing topics they choose match the criteria above.

Before you head out to select a few topics of your own, there is one thing that you must note - being polarizing doesn't necessarily mean that you have to be bold. It might be as simple as taking a stance against a specific ingredient used by your competitors, or calling out the gaps and issues in what they do and how they do it. It might even be as simple as supporting an event that your ideal customers might care about, or raising money for a charity or cause that has significance for you.

It certainly can mean that you're bold – like supporting a highly political cause – but it doesn't *have* to be that way. In fact, for most businesses, the subtle polarity aligned to the three criteria in the list above will be best.

A Glimpse Behind The Curtains Of Personal Life

At this moment, if you were to think of someone in your industry or market who is playing the "know the owner" game well, the chances are good that you'll know a bit about that person; a bit about their family life, a bit about their backstory and where they came from, a bit about how they came to do what they do, a bit about how they're different from others, and maybe a bit about what, or who, they personally like or don't like.

That's all on purpose. You know these things about them because they intentionally chose to share it with you… for business reasons.

Trust me, they don't do it because they want everyone and their mom to know their personal business (not many people want that). They do it because they understand that their story adds a layer of personality to their business that they can't otherwise get. This personality gives them a competitive edge and level of value that makes the business different from every other business in their industry. It also gives them a way to *unlink* their business from their actual products and services <u>so that the business becomes MORE</u> <u>than just its products and services.</u>

When customers and prospects feel as though they know not just who the owner is, but know <u>"who" the owner *IS*</u>, they are more likely to relate to them… and buy from them.

Not just that, but they also tend to be willing to pay higher prices for the goods and services that they offer. Kind of like how they are willing to pay more to support a friend than they are a big nameless, faceless, corporation that they can't relate to in the slightest.

The fact that customers relate to the owner increases the value of what the business sells. This helps to de-commoditize its products and services.

Relatability is the key here, and a glimpse into your personal life – through stories about things that make you human – is the most effective way to create the *"they're kinda like me"* phenomenon that drive customers to unlink your products and services from what they are so that you can attach a deeper value to what you do.

Curating The Story That Is Told When You're Not Around

Have you ever heard about a business because someone that you know, or someone who you follow/pay attention to, talks about them?

This happens all the time, and for many businesses, it is one of their best marketing channels. The leads and new customers that come to their business through the "I heard about you" path convert at higher rates, spend more money, and stay with the business longer.

To understand why, we must look at the psychology behind the matter. When a person mentions another business that they themselves like and recommend, there are a few psychological truths that come into play for the person listening to them:

1. They already have an established level of trust in the person making the comments and because of this they naturally have a higher level of trust that transfers over to your business.

2. The initial "will this work for me?" question is already answered because somebody who they relate to (the "influencer") says that it works. Therefore, they more naturally trust that it will work for them as well.

3. There is an element of "status" in following the lead of the person they follow or look up to. They look up to them in a way, even if they're just a friend, and want to do many of the things they do. As such, being more like them by using your product or service elevates the customer's sense of self-worth.

There are a range of additional elements of psychology that come into play here as well, but these three are, for the most part, the most important. It is for these reasons that the new customer lowers their guard initially (they trust in their purchase more) and remain a customer for longer (they want to be more like the person they follow or look up to). This drives them to convert at higher rates, spend more money, and remain a customer for longer.

It's an ideal situation for any business. One that should warrant an effort by a business owner to control and influence. At the very least, you should work to curate the story that others tell about you and your business. Put the words in their mouth so that when they tell someone else about you, the things that you want them to know is conveyed. Strangely, this is quite easy to do.

Even though influencing what others say and do, from the outside, might seem an insurmountable task, it is quite simple when you get to the root of it. Human beings communicate best through story and testimonial, <u>and they will repeat the stories and testimonials that you share with them</u>. So, if you control the stories and curate the testimonials, you will curate the story that is shared when you're not around. All you need to do is make sure that you have good stories and testimonials… and that you infuse them into your communications over and over again so that you sear every word into your customer's mind. That will then be the story that they tell about your business.

If you'd like more learning on how to tell better stories in your business then there is no better person to learn from than business legend, Dan Kennedy. His "Making Them Believe" course available ONLY through Magnetic Marketing Diamond membership is one that every business owner should complete.

Again, instead of myself pretending to be the authority on the topic, I'll simply direct you to Dan's diamond membership signup at the QR code below. Go ahead and scan it if you'd like to learn how to tell better stories (among many, many, other best-of-the-best business lessons that Dan offers):

RECESSION PROOF

An Experience Unlike Any Other.

RECESSION PROOF

THE STRATEGY

Lackluster. That's the experience delivered to customers by the vast majority of businesses. They process transactions and deliver promised goods and services without much thought as to what the customer's experience is.

Case in point, on a recent Saturday I visited six different businesses as I ran around town doing errands. Nothing extravagant, just six everyday errands at six everyday local small businesses. I got a haircut, went to the grocery store, grabbed a few things at a local sports store, picked up takeout from my wife's favorite Mexican restaurant, picked up a piece of furniture from a local dealer, and grabbed a coffee at a drive-thru stand.

As you can likely imagine based on your own experience with doing these types of everyday errands, there wasn't much that was special to the day. The barber who cut my hair sat me in a chair, faced me towards a TV, and then proceeded to mindlessly trim what's left of my wavy brown locks. The grocery store clerk that rang me up swiped and scanned my food without saying much more than "How are you today?". The teenage worker at the sports store practically ran to the back warehouse when I tried to ask him a question. The server at the restaurant handed me my bag of food and then eagerly checked the receipt to see what kind of tip I left. The furniture dealer took my name and then said "Yeah, it's over there" while pointing to a box in the corner... that I then had to pick up and load myself. The barista took my order, sloshed around some coffee and steamed milk, and then shoved her arm out the window with cup in hand before robotically saying "have a nice day!".

By no means did I expect anything more than what I got at these establishments. That's just how it is in today's world, I _expect_ a lackluster, subpar, lazy, and often rude experience at most businesses that I visit.

In a good economy, this lackluster customer experience isn't much of a big deal. Customers will come and go, and the business will continue on without much of a worry as to who's coming in through their doors (or website), how they got there, and if they'll ever come back. There is a glut of customers who will come simply because of low supply and high demand.

Transition into a tough economy, however, and the story changes. Supply increases across both products and services, demand for all of it shrinks, and – almost all of a sudden – _EVERY_ customer matters. How they came to you matters, how much money they spent with you matters, what they purchased (and the margins on it) matters, and whether or not they will become a repeat customer matters (a lot).

As such, the experience that each and every customer has with a business becomes a top-level priority. It becomes simply unacceptable to have a person, any person, leave your business thinking to themselves "Meh, it was _okay_ service", "Yeah, I _guess_ they were okay", "The product did a _decent enough_ job for me", or <u>any other version of **_indifferent_** thought</u>.

That's because…

Your Customers <u>CANNOT</u> Be Indifferent To Your Business

Indifference – the lack of enthusiasm, or even care, for your business – is a plague that, if left untreated, will drain the lifeforce (profitability) from your ledgers. Customers will come, and customers will go. There will be no loyalty. No attachment to your business. Nothing except mindless, almost meaningless, transactions (much like the ones I made in my examples).

Over time, the difficulty of customer acquisition will increase – as it always does in recessions – and those mindless transactions will become more and more expensive for a business to get, and retention of customers will become increasingly important.

So, how do you retain more customers?

An <u>exceptional customer experience</u> will be the first place to start. Customers who have a good experience with a business are more likely to return. Customers who have an *exceptional* experience are more likely to return, spend more money, *and* tell their friends. For that reason, an *exceptional* customer experience should be, and must be, your goal.

But here's the thing…

A Good Customer Experience Can Be Actualized In An Instant. An EXCEPTIONAL Customer Experience Can Only Be Actualized <u>Over Time.</u>

If you're thinking that customer experience is something that happens only at the time of a transaction, or immediately after, think again. Sure, what happens at the time of a transaction and immediately afterwards – when the customer is excited about what they just purchased – is important… but it's not as important as what happens <u>before</u> and <u>after</u> the transaction.

That said, let's take a look at the tactics that will help you to craft the perfect pre-sale and post-sale experience.

THE TACTICS:

The Experience Leading Up To The Sale

Too often, business owners focus efforts on one of two things:

1. Getting more customers to buy
2. Getting more customers to buy *again*

While these are good and noble goals for any business, the obsessive focus on them without thought to the customer's journey is a cardinal sin when it comes to customer experience.

We've all experienced an overly eager salesperson who *clearly* only wanted you to buy from them for selfish reasons – they wanted your money and could have cared less about you as a person or the results you'd get from the product or service that they sell you. They are *indifferent to you*, thinking to themselves "Meh, another ~~victim~~ customer, another dollar".

As such, your experience leading up to the sale in these situations likely leads you to think "I'm never, ever, not in a million years, buying from *that* place"... or.... "I'm never, ever, not in a million years, buying from *that* place *again*". Either way, despite your purchasing decision made in the moment, you are lost to that business as a long-term customer because your experience *leading up* to the sale did not meet your expectations. It certainly didn't make you feel all warm and fuzzy inside. Quite the opposite, in fact.

Here's the unfortunate and difficult-to-hear truth – many businesses, without realizing it, repeat the mistakes of that slimy salesperson <u>by treating their customers with indifference</u>. No, that doesn't mean that they are overly pushy, rude, and selfish like the salesperson in the example provided, but that they don't leave their prospective customers with the warm and fuzzy feeling that makes them feel happy about their buying experience. <u>The business' indifference leads to their customers' indifference.</u>

Read that one again, and then five times fast: *The business' indifference leads to their customers' indifference.*

It's simple cause and effect where the business' lack of differentiating action leads to a lackluster and forgettable customer experience. They put in little to no effort to make the customer buying journey *exceptional*. Nothing to make it stand out or otherwise trigger the customer to stop and think "Wow, this place is really earning every dollar I'm about to give them... and more".

<u>**Customers NEED to think that your business is earning every dollar that they spend with you, and more**</u>. If they do not think this way then it becomes much too easy for them to begin comparing your

business to every other provider on the market, which is the early stages of commoditization. That's why this is so important. An exceptional pre-sale buying experience is a key factor in differentiating your business and justifying higher costs/higher margins. The experience is a part of the *value* added on top of your products and/or services.

But that's not all. Because a customer's experience *before* the sale has a direct impact on their experience *after*. If they do not have the "wow" factor on the front-end then you'll be fighting an uphill battle to get them to feel happy and excited about becoming a repeat customer – which should always be the ultimate goal.

Creating an exceptional pre-sale buying experience, fortunately, isn't all that hard. It all boils down to infusing some of the following elements into your sales process (online or offline):

1. **Create the "Entryway Affirmation" experience**: Create a setting, specific to your business, that makes your customer think "Oh yeah, I'm *definitely* in the right place" when they come to your store, website, stand, etc. They need to be *affirmed* that the decision to visit your business was the right decision at that exact moment in time.

2. **Make them feel valued**: Take away any question that you appreciate them for being there. Treat them like an A-lister who means the world to your business (without smothering them or being insincere).

3. **Anticipate their needs before they ask**: Put yourself in your customer's shoes for a moment when they are visiting your business and think through what they might need and want. Give them *that* before they have to ask.
   *more on this topic later in this chapter.

4. **Make the buying experience an actual experience**: Give your customers something to remember by creating an experience that is fun and enjoyable. By doing so, you substantially improve not only their buying experience, but their loyalty and referability, among many other benefits for your business.

A great example of this is the Build-A-Bear Workshop business model, which is entirely built around the *experience* of getting hands-on with their products and services before the customer ever has to pay a dime.

Another example is a coffee roasting client of mine who offers his customers the experience of choosing the green beans from the grower(s) of their choice, setting the duration and heat for roasting, and then crafting up their own personal label. I've seen versions of this in the wine/vineyard industry, custom car industry, and a range of others.

5. **Understand Preferences**: Don't ask someone what they are looking for or would like, ask about their preferences – what they prefer and what they don't prefer. Ask them detailed questions so that you understand what they are really looking for (and not just the generic thing that they tell you they are looking for).

   In professional sales, they call this "probing questions" and in professional marketing they call it a "customer survey". Whichever you call it, and whichever is most applicable to your business, the outcome is the same – you make a recommendation based on their preferences for what they should buy. As a result, they feel like they are special… and not like they are just another order.

   This step might not apply if you're presentation selling (selling from a stage, through a webinar, or other one-to-many setting).

6. **Create a low-pressure sales environment, but give them a reason to act NOW**: Nobody likes to feel *pressured* to make a decision in a moment… but businesses also can't afford to lose potential customers who leave and never return. It's one of the central dichotomies in all of business. While there is no perfect solution to appease both sides of the coin, there is a compromise in creating a low-pressure sales environment but giving customers a very compelling, time-sensitive, reason to buy immediately.

   Often times, the best approach here is to make customers a very enticing, practically irresistible, offer that must be accepted within a set period of time. It might be within the hour, or it might be within the month, but there is a definitive and non-flexible timestamp by which a decision (and purchase) must be made. This offer itself puts pressure on the customer to buy *instead* of the business putting pressure on them.

7. **Incentivize keeping in contact**: Even with a phenomenal offer in front of them, not all customers will buy right away. They need time, and that's okay. While the time-sensitive offer made to them should expire if they walk away, that doesn't mean that you should give up on them.

   It's perfectly fine to give customers the time that they need to make decisions, but it is not okay to give them "space" to escape (figuratively, not literally). This means that you need to get a means to contact them after they leave so that you can continue the sales discussion.

   The best way to do this is to incentivize them to maintain contact and continue the discussion over a longer sales cycle. Put in simpler words, **bribe them** with something they are likely to want in exchange for 1)their contact information and 2)their agreement and permission to have you follow up with them in X hours/days/weeks. Yes, this fully means that you should be giving them something of value in exchange for keeping the discussion going.

   Many times, and especially if advertising, this step can come before step 6. More on that in Part 2 of this book.

8. **Make A Recommendation, With Options, Including A Competitor**: As mentioned in the last bullet, making a recommendation based on preferences is necessary for a good buying experience. How you make that recommendation is also just as important.

   Customers need and want to feel like they have options, so give them options, preferably at low, medium, and high price tiers. But, if you can, don't just limit the options to what you offer. Surprise them by also suggesting an option offered by one of your competitors (unless you're making the offer in a "captive" setting, like ordering while seated at a restaurant).

This might seem counterintuitive, but by recommending alternative options it shows that you have confidence in what you do, how much you charge, and why they should buy from you.

By infusing some or all of these tactics into your pre-sales process, you can improve your customer's buying experience in a way that influences the rest of their relationship with you. If done correctly, this will be a superpower within your business that allows you to create raving fans while making it hard for your competitors to keep up with you.

Delivery: Don't Drop The Ball

If you've crafted an exceptional pre-sale experience for your customers then the actual delivery of your products and services should, for the most part, be set up for success. The customer will already be excited, bought in, and ready to tell the world about their experience.

Problem is, you can still drop the ball, and many do... especially if there is any waiting time between when they purchase and when you actually deliver the product, service, _or final result_. The longer the wait is, the bigger the risk will be that you might drop the ball.

For example, homebuilders are notorious for this. They get their customers extremely excited about their purchase during the pre-sale and sale phase... and then, typically, drop the ball during the delivery phase. They head off and get to work for months, or even years, and leave their customer high and dry while waiting for delivery of what they've purchased. With just a few updates provided along the way, they almost forget that the home they are building _is for their customer_ and that they need to keep the excitement going until they hand over the keys (and then some).

PART 1 – CUSTOMER OBSESSION

Enterprise software – the type that businesses purchase and then take weeks, months, or years to "configure" before they can use it – is another area where this happens. The customer has to go through an extended waiting period before they get to actually experience the product. Worse yet, they have to go through a waiting period where issues tend to come up and people tend to mess up. These problems are notorious for aggravating the customer and making them question their decision to purchase from the software company that they selected.

While the examples provided here might not apply to your specific business, they were provided for a reason – to highlight real world examples of *long* delivery cycles where a customer might be lost to the business. They are somewhat on the extreme of delivery length but that just highlights some of the things that can go wrong:

- Customers can feel "forgotten about."
- Issues that arise between the time they buy and when they get their final result can make customers second guess their purchasing decision.
- You/your people can mess up, miss things, or say things that shouldn't be said.
- Customers can lose enthusiasm and become more critical of what your business is or isn't doing to their satisfaction.

Understanding the things that can go wrong between the time of purchase and the time when customers get the final result that they've paid for is imperative to getting ahead of these issues and keeping your customers engaged and happy throughout this phase. Oftentimes, these are the things most overlooked in a business, so calling them out is a necessity.

That said, if your business has any time more than a few minutes where your customer is waiting then you should find ways to keep them engaged, distracted, or entertained so that their experience remains a good one. And, to provide a few examples of what you might do:

- If you own a restaurant and have customers waiting between when they order and when they get their food, you might have a band, singer, or piano playing to entertain them. Or, maybe you have a signature game that is unique to your business at every table.

- If you own a software company and have a configuration period then you might find ways to provide value for your client while your team does the configuration work.

- If you own an ecomm store where customers have to wait for shipping, you might have an entertaining video series about all the ways to use *and not use* the product that is drip emailed to them in the days between order and delivery.
  Bonus points for infusing humor or other emotions relevant to your product into the series.

The list of what you might do is nearly endless, and that's a good thing. Moral of the story here is simply that you should be doing *something* to fill the time between purchase and delivery/fulfillment. What you actually do is in your hands now.

After The Sale: Shock And Awe Onboarding

I reference legendary marketing and business guru Dan Kennedy a lot, and for good reason, as the man might just be the best small business mind of all time. The reason that I bring this up is because this next tactic was learned 100% from him – shock and awe onboarding.

The premise that Dan teaches on this topic is that whenever you have a new customer come into your business, it is in <u>your</u> best interest to blow them away with a phenomenal, almost unheard of, onboarding process. Why? Because a customer's first interaction with your business sets the tone for their level of enthusiasm for your business from that point forward. If they are amazed, you will be rewarded with long term benefits of them as a customer.

Dan takes it as far as preaching that you must <u>*invest*</u> in your new customers instead of looking at them as a source of revenue. What that means, and what he often preaches, is that...

The Person Who Can <u>Spend The Most</u> To Acquire A Customer WINS<u>.</u>

This is contrary to what most business owners believe and practice. In their minds, they want to *cut* the cost of customer acquisition and onboarding, not increase it. But that's a fool's errand, and here's why – **a customer acquired on the cheap is most often of low value to the business**. They typically don't spend much and are much more likely to look for commoditized products and services. Said another way, cheap-to-acquire customers are often bargain hunters who will jump ship to the cheapest offers on the market when given the opportunity. They are also more likely to be the customers that give you the most headaches with complaints, returns/refunds, and all the rest that you most definitely don't want in your business.

Conversely, customers that take a bit more effort, and often money, to bring into your business have a much higher value potential over the long term. They are more likely to fit with your Ideal Customer Profile (ICP) and be looking for products and/or services just like yours on a recurring basis. They are also more likely to spend more and stay longer; all traits that you want in customers that you serve.

Naturally, if you're going to invest in acquiring new customers then it is in your best interest to intentionally and systematically go after the customers who are most likely to become your best and most loyal customers over the long term. Cheap customers are not worth the effort, cost, or bandwidth… unless of course you're 100% okay with playing the commoditized game of business.

That said, it is wise to invest in giving your best customers the best experience possible on the front end so that you hook them as "diehards" of your business. That means giving them an exceptional pre-sales, delivery period, and post-sale experience. The post-sale experience is where the shock and awe onboarding comes in.

Once you've delivered your product or service, and would normally walk away, is the exact moment that you should go "all-in" on surprising your new customer with an unexpected bonus. After all, this is your chance to hook them and turn them into customers for life.

To provide a couple examples of this:

- I have a friend in the real estate business who delivers quarterly gifts to his customers for TWO YEARS after he's helped them either sell or buy a home. As a result of this, he has the largest and most successful brokerage in the area. His customers refuse to work with anyone else, and they refer him to everyone they know who might be either buying or selling.

- One of my friends in the software industry sends all of his new customers a shock and awe box to their homes that has t-shirts, stickers, coffee mugs, books, and a bunch of other goodies. He also then sends them a monthly print newsletter with articles helping them to get the most out of their subscription to his software, as well as just generally improve in their business.

In both of these cases, and in about a dozen more that I could offer, the business owner is **investing in their new customer**. They recognize that the lifetime value (LTV) of the new customer is higher if they themselves put a bit more effort into giving them an exceptional post-sale experience. This small investment – that almost NOBODY else in their industry does – provides their business with benefits that far exceed their return-on-investment expectations.

Needs Met Without Having To Ask

I recently visited a Ford dealership in Sarasota, FL where I had to wait about an hour for my truck to get a routine service. Upon checking in, they greeted me with upbeat personalities, hooked me up with a "coupon" for a smoothie at their café, gave me a guided tour of their (very nice) waiting area, and then topped it off by sitting me in a hydro massage chair where I could relax for 20 minutes before heading back over to the café to get my smoothie.

I never had to ask for a thing. They *anticipated* that I might get hungry, so they gave me a smoothie. They *anticipated* that I might get uncomfortable sitting in a waiting room for an hour, so they put me in a massage chair. They *anticipated* that I might get a bit grumpy by having to wait, so they greeted me with upbeat and happy personalities. They *anticipated* my needs without me having to ask for a thing.

Overall, they created an experience that took the service they were offering to an entirely different level. They were no longer just changing the oil in my truck, <u>they were creating an enjoyable experience that I wouldn't get anywhere else</u>. At my next oil change, you can best believe that they were the ones to get my business. There are LOTS of options on the market for oil changes, but there is only one Sarasota Ford.

Now, I know that you might be thinking – the experience they delivered sounds expensive. Right?

Wrong.

Expensive is a relative term in business. When looked at from the perspective of cost per appointment, I'm sure that their costs to provide this type of experience – especially in the locale where they reside – is higher than what other dealerships have for the same service. However, when looked at from the perspective of evaluating likelihood that their clients…

1. Become repeat, and long-term, customers

2. Tell others about their experience

3. Choose to buy their next vehicle there

… and the "cost" per appointment is quickly, and definitively, outweighed by the benefits reaped. In short, you get back what you put into your customer's experience. That's the takeaway here –

invest in your customers, anticipate their needs, and they will most often return the favor, plus some.

"Random" Acts Of Staying In Touch

In one of his weekly faxes sent to his Diamond level members, Dan Kennedy pulled back the curtain in his business to reveal something profound – the seemingly random, somewhat personalized, messages and/or letters that his customers would get from him were in fact… planned.

Instead of sending "blah" mass marketing to his customers – like most businesses do – he sent individualized touchpoint messages to each of his customers on an intermittent basis. These would be links to articles relevant to their business, or the old "I saw that you _____ " messages referencing something they had recently done, or even just (seemingly) random thoughts that he had that they might like to know about.

His customers felt as though he, someone that they looked up to, was paying attention to *them*.

By taking mere moments of his time to make his customers feel as though they were important enough for him to take time out of his busy schedule to think about them embedded something that many business owners forget about in today's day and age – relationship.

Remember how earlier in this book we covered the topic of "knowing the owner"? Well, what Dan does here with his intermittent check ins is flipping the script and saying "I know you too!". He's making the customer's relationship with the business two-way instead of one-way. Brilliance.

So, if you're not already doing "random" acts of keeping in touch with your customers then you might be missing out on one of the most profound tools you have available to you – a relationship with those who give you money.

The Unique Advantage You Didn't Know You Had

According to a *U.S. News and World Report*, the average American business loses around 15% of their customer base each and every year. Of this 15%:

- 68% are lost to a competitor due to poor or indifferent service.
- 14% leave because of a dispute or complaint that was unsatisfactorily resolved.
- 9% leave because of price.
- 5% were referred/recommended elsewhere, and
- 1% die

That means that 82% of lost customers, based on the top 2 reasons above, are leaving because of a customer experience issue. Their experience was either indifferent, poor, or downright bad. In this, lies your advantage.

If your competitors are losing ~15% of their customers each and every year during a good economy, then you can best bet that they'll be losing a heck of a lot more than that during a recession. Each and every customer that they lose is an opportunity for you.

When times get tough, many businesses go into protectionist mode, often at the expense of their customers. It almost never fails, businesses across all industries begin looking for ways that they can protect their bottom line. They cut the perks that they offer, lower their quality, make it more difficult to request a return, and generally find ways to "short" the customer wherever they can so that they can protect their margins while playing the game of having the lowest price in town. It's a losing game... but we won't tell them that.

By centering your business around a customer obsession, you will have the advantage of being the business that your competitors' customers look to switch to. Not all of them, of course, but the good ones. We're talking about the non-price shoppers that value a good experience and are willing to pay a fair premium for it. Those are the customers that you want anyways.

But that's not the only advantage that you'll get. An exceptional customer experience will also help you to combat customer loss/churn in your own business. Remember, on average, 82% of customers leave a business because of an indifferent, poor, or outright bad customer experience.

This means that if you truly have an exceptional customer experience then you can reduce your customer churn down to just 2.7%. Here's the math:

$$82\% \text{ of } 15\% = 12.3\%$$

*% of total churn, showing overall customer loss due to a poor experience

$$15\% - 12.3\% = 2.7\%$$

*total churn (15%) minus % saved by having an exception customer experience

To make these numbers feel more realistic, and to make the math look, well, less "mathy", let's look at the numbers in an imaginary business that has 1000 customers annually, each worth an average of $1000/year to the business - making this a $1M/year business.

If the business has an average churn of 15% of customers each year, then they lose 150 customers annually. At $1000/year average spend for each customer, this equates to $150,000/year in lost revenue. That's a fairly hefty revenue loss... but it's not the whole picture. Every customer lost must be replaced, otherwise the business will shrivel and die. So, if we assume that it costs the business on average $100 to acquire each new customer then the replacement cost for those they lose annually adds another $15,000, bringing the cost of total annual losses to $165,000 (16.5% of the total annual revenue of $1M).

Many of my peers in the business consulting space would argue that this is just the tip of the iceberg of what the losses are, and they're absolutely right. There _are_ other losses that can be factored into this equation that will make the numbers look a lot worse... but, for simplicity's sake, we'll leave it at $165,000 for now.

PART 1 – CUSTOMER OBSESSION

I don't know about you, but I certainly don't want to lose 16.5% of my annual revenue each and every year because I got lazy on the customer experience that I deliver. That just seems too much like lighting money on fire for me.

That said, let's look at what the numbers look like at the opposite end of the spectrum in a business that has an exceptional customer experience, enjoying a 2.7% churn:

1000 customers x 2.7% = 27 customers lost annually

27 x $1000 avg value = $27,000 revenue lost annually

27 x $100 replacement cost = $2700 replacement costs

$2700 + $27,000 = $29,700 total annual revenue loss due to churn (just 2.97% of total annual revenue)

That's a difference of $135,300 in revenue (13.53% of the total annual revenue of $1M). This is revenue that can be _saved_, each year, by having an exceptional customer experience. Revenue, that for the most part, and depending on your business model, goes mostly to your bottom line.

Are you starting to see the advantage of having an exceptional customer experience?

RECESSION PROOF

An Exclusive Club, With Perks

RECESSION PROOF

THE STRATEGY

Have you ever been a member of a hard-to-get-into group that you were proud to be a part of? Maybe it was a small, tight knit, mastermind. Maybe it was a membership at a vineyard where you had your own section of vines reserved just for your own private label wine. Maybe it was a gaming or sporting group where members were given exclusive releases and access to experiences. Maybe it was a top-notch restaurant that only members were allowed to dine at. Maybe it was simply a store rewards program where you racked up points that actually meant something in terms of perks (and not just discounts).

Whatever it was, if it was done well then you likely felt more attached to that business: more loyal, more open to spending money, and more satisfied with your purchases. Those are the very reasons that we are covering this topic at this point in the book. Memberships – good ones – are one of the best drivers of long-term customer engagement, satisfaction, and loyalty that a business can employ.

It's important to note, however, that not all memberships are marketed *as* memberships at all. Instead, they are made more simple - like perks offered only to top level clients, or special access granted only to a select few customers. Most often, though, these memberships are exactly what they sound like – paid admittance into a group that receives special status and benefits from a business.

Either way, the concept is the same – **you are a member of an exclusive group that *makes you feel connected* to the business that is offering it**.

Stop for a moment and think about what you just read; a group, corralled by a business, who is *given good reason* to remain a customer and *not* look anywhere else because they feel *connected* to the business. This is a profound concept, and one that many of the world's most successful business leaders covet. Warren Buffett calls it "moat building", Dan Kennedy "herd building", and Seth Godin "tribe building".

Whatever you call it, the business that does this is much like a rancher rounding up their cattle and driving them into a pen where they are fed, kept happy, and *prevented* from wandering off where another rancher might snatch them up. No, that doesn't mean that you should look at your customers as cattle, but that you should look at the similarities between the processes. Round 'em up and build a fence to keep them… because your competitors are *constantly* trying to steal them from you.

That brings us to the point of, and reason for, this chapter…

Protecting Your Customers From The Other Businesses Who Are Trying To Steal/Poach Them From You Is Imperative.

The Best Way To Protect Them Is To <u>Give Them A Compelling Reason</u> To Be Faithful To Your Business, And Only Your Business, By Creating An <u>Exclusive</u> Group For Them To Be A Part Of.

When done correctly, customers who consider themselves "members" of a group facilitated or created by a business have an **emotional** connection to that business. That emotional connection leads them to feel as though they must be, and want to be, somewhat exclusive with that business. Strangely, this is much like what is seen in romantic relationships… minus the romance… but you get the point. The customer feels as though they are a part of something, and therefore tell themselves that they must be faithful to the business.

For example:

- Members of elite membership-only restaurants gain a feeling of status from their membership and choose to eat at that restaurant more often than any other.

- Members of Inner Circle masterminds – real in-person ones that can be hard to get into – have a connection to their mastermind and tend to prioritize the time they invest in it over other groups they might be a part of.

- Members of diamond tier hotel and/or airline programs tend to use that hotel or airline almost exclusively.

- Members of VIP home maintenance clubs – ones that offer proactive preventive services that they make sure customers use – feel protected and "covered" and have some of the best loyalty and referrals in the industry.

The reason that many large corporations use memberships, like the hotel/airline example, is because they work. As members move up the loyalty tier, and gain more benefits for doing so, they become more and more loyal to the business and are much less open to trying out any other alternatives. This is no different for small businesses. It's just a rarer sight to see small businesses implementing the strategy of memberships (which is a shame… and an *opportunity* for you).

But before we dive into how to capitalize on that opportunity, it's important to make the distinction here that a membership and a subscription are very different things (that are often mixed up). A subscription is simply a recurring payment for a product or service, whereas a membership is inclusion in a group that carries meaning and often offers perks.

Simply giving your customers a subscription will not be cause for them to have a connection to your business. They might, but it's certainly not a given. Memberships, on the other hand, carry a deeper meaning than just a product or service being delivered, and are very powerful mechanisms for creating a connection for, and between, customers and a business.

Now, with that clarification, let's cover the tactics involved in creating and managing a membership program in your business...

THE TACTICS:

The Perks Of Membership

Often times, when business owners think about creating a membership, they have an immense feeling of overwhelm. They don't have enough time available to build out something like that, never mind run it. And the costs of it, don't even get started on that!

It's not that they don't see the benefits of having their best customers more loyal to their business, because they do. They just can't fathom how in the world they would dream up what it might look like and/or manage everything that it entails to keep it running. It's too much.

"Maybe in the future", is what they tell themselves.

The thing is, creating a membership doesn't have to mean that you create big and elaborate membership programs right out of the gate. Not in the slightest. A simple club that offers members exclusive perks that they couldn't otherwise get is all that is needed to start.

Here are a few examples of what you might do as a first step in your journey to creating a membership:

- Tell your best customers – the ones who have been coming to you the longest – that you appreciate their business and have marked them in your system as VIP. As a result, any time that they call or come in they will be given priority treatment. They'll also get a complimentary _____ (whatever makes sense for your business to give as a perk).

  Once you have your best customers as "members" of the exclusive group, begin telling all of your customers – new and old – that you've implemented a VIP loyalty program and they can get _____ if they _____ (fill in the blanks with what's included in the VIP program, and what the requirements are for them to qualify and maintain it).

- Set new hours of operation where certain times of the day are reserved for "Gold" members – typically your most popular times of the day – and other times of the day are "open" hours.

  In order for customers to get a "Gold" membership they must pay a subscription fee (or higher level subscription fee). In return, they get access during the preferred time along with a range of other perks that you throw in to make the _value_ of the membership seem like a reasonable deal for the price (but not too good of a deal, otherwise everyone will take it, and you want some exclusivity here).

  Of course, you'll need to communicate to your existing customer base well in advance that this change will be going into effect so that you give them a chance to sign up and don't alienate them.

- Create an _experience_ related to your business that only members can book. This might be a "brew your own beer" experience if you're a brewery, or a "meet a celebrity" party annually if you're a service-based provider ("celebrity" can simply be someone well known in your industry, like an author or influencer).

Naturally, the better the perks are that you offer, the more interest you will have from customers to join. And if you don't have customers engaging in your membership program then improve the perks until you see it start to take off.

An Alternative Membership

An alternative type of membership program is the type where ONLY members can be customers, and you _must_ be a paying member before you can be a customer. This is the Costco model of membership, and it is worth considering in your business.

That's because, in this model, you are _forcing_ potential customers to raise their hand and say "yes, what you are offering is 100% for me". They are not dabbling or dipping their toe in the waters of what you offer, they _know_ that they are a customer and want the exclusive perks that you're offering. If they aren't 100% sold that they fit the mold of your business then they won't become a member.

The beauty of this model is that it has quite a few benefits for the business that are otherwise difficult to come by. For example:

- It creates a natural filter in your business whereby most bad customers – the kind that you wish wouldn't visit your business – don't become customers in the first place. Only the customers that truly identify with, and align to, your business become paying members.

  These people tend to have a better understanding of the realities in your industry and are more likely to become your diehard customers that will carry your business through good and bad economies.

- The membership dues create a baseline revenue that you can use to cover base operating expenses. Many businesses that employ this membership model even use their base operating expenses divided by their target membership count as the pricing strategy for the membership.

- Marketing becomes much simpler, as nearly all of your marketing can be focused around the benefits of membership instead of the benefits of a given product or service. Your best customers will resonate with the benefits of the membership and your marketing will make them think "this is for me".

- Members like to talk about their membership… and tend to talk to others who are just like them. Referrals to your business are naturally infused into these discussions about the membership.

As you can imagine, the benefits of this type of membership are many. I'd even go as far as to argue that, for most businesses, this type of membership is what they should transition to as a core strategy for weathering an economic storm. I say this because…

> # Arguably, The Most Important Aspect Of A Business During Tough Economic Times Is A Robust Base Of Diehard Customers...

… and this membership model is one of the best ways to create customers who will stick with you through thick and thin (in most businesses).

That's not to say that it is the only membership option, or the right option for every business, but that it's a highly effective one for most businesses. With that said, in the event that the Costco style membership model doesn't work for your business then some of the more simple membership options that we started with can be employed as strategy to create an increasing amount of diehard customers.

The Affluent Rule The Economic Roost, In Good Economies & Bad

One of the biggest mistakes that business owners make is thinking that a customer is a customer, and that all should be treated the same. They shouldn't.

The harsh reality of this world is that, economically, people are not equal. She/he who has more money in their bank account available to spend on goods and services is worth more to a business than he/she who does not have money. This is just simple, undebatable, fact. The affluent are better customers than the poor... and should be treated as such.

Smart business owners take the time to understand what the affluent people in their industry and market want so that they can tailor their business' offerings around that. This isn't just because the affluent have money to spend, as that's only part of the reason that they are better customers.

Affluent people have a tendency to want less hassle in their lives and are willing to pay a premium to the business that removes that hassle. The old saying "rich people don't own a shovel, they *hire* a shovel" is true as true could be. They don't want to be bothered with the inconveniences that "regular" people put up with. They want higher quality with less headaches in everything that they purchase. This is true in both the products and services that they buy.

The reason that I bring this up at this point in the book is because, in most cases, **membership programs should be geared towards what the affluent in your industry and market want**. The membership is, after all, intended to have some exclusivity to it.

So, if the affluent in your market want to have access to your business without the hassle of crowds, lines, or waiting then make that one of the benefits of your membership. If they want someone to bring the product or service to their door, add *that* as a benefit. If they want to have the social standing of being a member that only caters to the elite, then make your membership *more* exclusive and expensive.

Obviously, you'll need to be realistic about what that you offer in your membership, as not *everything* that the affluent want will be possible for you. As much as you can, though, you should be tailoring your membership program to serve the affluent.

A <u>Print</u> Newsletter They Look Forward To

One of the most powerful, yet underutilized, tools that a business has available to it is an old-fashioned print newsletter. Yes, print. Not a digital magazine. Not a PDF'd guide attached to an email. Print.

PART 1 – CUSTOMER OBSESSION

Something that your members can hold in their hands and look forward to getting in the mail each month.

It might seem so simple – too simple – but a print newsletter is an amazing tool for keeping your best customers engaged and in the know about what's happening at your business. For a just couple of dollars per month, a print newsletter allows you to get in front of your customers in a way that they remember. That's benefit #1. But that's not the only benefit.

The content within the newsletter gives you a chance to tell them more about you and what's happening in your life (further embedding their belief that they "know the owner"), while also giving you a chance to indoctrinate them on why what you do is so much better than your competitors. No other media format offers this kind of opportunity.

But, again, that's not all.

Often times, a print newsletter can be included as one of the benefits of a membership. That means that it is a paid-for product that allows you to be in front of your best customers every single month. If you're reading between the lines here, this means that it doesn't cost you a dime to do ongoing and consistent marketing to your customers. You can subtly and almost covertly introduce new products and services, upsell and cross-sell them on things that they haven't yet tried, all while keeping in constant contact with them in a way that is so much better than email (which tend to be deleted quickly).

But, still, that's not all.

Statistically speaking, customers who receive print newsletters in the mail are more likely to refer your business to friends, family, and associates. Sometimes they gift your newsletter to another, other times, they share the stories and examples they pick up from your newsletter in conversations with peers, and other times yet, they speak highly of your business as the leader in your market simply because you are the one business that is most visible to them. They refer because they feel connected to your business, largely as a result of your constant, high-quality, communication with them in the form of a print newsletter.

But, one last time, that's not all.

Strangely, or maybe not so strangely, customers that receive a print newsletter tend to have fewer objections and less resistance to the offers that you present to them. From my own business, I can attest that conversions on offers made to newsletter recipients are quite substantially higher than the conversions of other existing customers (who don't receive a newsletter), prospects that are on my lead list, and cold traffic that randomly finds my sites and offers.

For all of these reasons, and more, newsletters are one of the most powerful tools that a business can use. In summary, a good newsletter allows your business to:

1. Remain in consistent contact with your customers in a format that is the most likely to be retained, read, and remembered.
2. Give your customers a deeper sense of "knowing the owner".
3. Keep them up to date on developments in your business, and what might be coming up that they can be excited for.
4. Indoctrinate them on the benefits of your business over others in the market.
5. Market to them for free, or at low cost; subtly introducing upsells and cross-sells.
6. Obtain more referrals to their family, friends, and associates.
7. Enhance their feelings of connection to your business.
8. Reduce objections and resistance to your offers so that you can increase conversions.

In my own business, for the reasons above and throughout this chapter, I flat out refuse to do any service-based work for anyone *unless* they have an annual subscription to my membership program, which is centered around my newsletter. If they want me to write a sales letter, or do the copy on their funnel, or write an email sequence, or provide business consultation, or do any other form of service for them then they are required to have an annual membership and receive my monthly newsletter.

The power of the membership program and newsletter is so profound that I have structured my entire business around it (much like Costco). Should you as well (in one form or another)?

Make Leaving Difficult & Heart Wrenching

Every membership on the face of this earth has a problem - people are free to leave whenever they feel like it, and many do. Some leave, and then come back, and then leave again. Others change the groups they are a part of at every changing of the seasons. Others, yet, have the gall to be a member for years only to cancel out of the blue and request a refund for *all* of the years they had been a member (yikes!).

This "problem" exists in nearly every membership program I have ever seen, even the ones that are *constantly* over delivering and providing an immense level of value. There is no membership that is "safe" from it. Every business that offers a membership simply has to deal with the realities of human nature in their customers.

But that doesn't mean that you have to lay down and take it. There are options for countering flaky customer behavior in your membership program. Here are just a few:

- **The Mafia Membership**: In the olden days, when a person joined the mafia (a.k.a. "The Mob") they had to make a lifelong commitment that they would never leave, ever. If for some reason they did leave, or even tried, there would be consequences.

  While the consequences that the mob doled out to their members who tried to leave are a bit extreme for an everyday modern business, the premise is not. There is absolutely no reason that a business can't institute a "member for life" policy whereby once a customer leaves they *cannot* return (at least without jumping through many, many, hoops to do so).

  By creating a finite policy that disincentivizes cancellation a business can tap into the psychological effects of Fear of Loss (FOL) and/or Fear of Missing Out (FOMO). Members don't want to lose something that they consider to bring value to their life, nor do they want to miss out on the opportunities brought about through their inclusion in the membership.

- **The Cancelation Offer**: At most businesses, when a customer goes to cancel their membership there is very little to no effort made by the business to save them from churning. They simply accept their cancellation at the time, and then send them a "we want you back" marketing message a few months later.

  This is a HUGE missed opportunity. At the time when a customer tries to cancel, there is a window of opportunity where you can ask what went wrong and if they'll give you an opportunity to fix it. Essentially, instead of saying "we want you back" in the future, you can say "we want you to stay and are willing to do what we can to fix it" in the moment.

  This simple "cancellation offer" can save a substantial percentage of your customers from churning out of your business.

- **The "It'll Cost You More" Membership**: Often times, customers can come and go in membership programs because there is no recourse for doing so. One of the simplest ways to prevent this is to increase your membership prices slightly (often 2x-3x) and then discount all *new* memberships. Then, when a member looks to leave, you simply remind them that they will have to pay full price if and when they return.

- **The "On Hold" Membership**: Sometimes, there are instances in people's lives where they need to put things that they normally enjoy on hold for a while. Maybe they're having a baby. Maybe they're in the military and are being deployed. Maybe they're going through a major family change. Whatever it is that they are going through doesn't matter. What matters is that you offer them an option to push pause and return later.

- **The Tiered Membership**: A great motivator for a customer to stick with a business (retention) is to have something to look forward to, move upwards to, and feel proud of. That's what tiered memberships do. At each level of the membership – from bronze all the way up to platinum, or whatever you decide to call your tiers – their retention rates increase alongside their brand loyalty. There is a sense of status in having the level of membership that they do, and they don't want to give this up.

Essentially, all of these strategies are mechanisms to make leaving your membership difficult and heart-wrenching. It's a form of reverse psychology that makes customers feel as though they'd be losing or missing out on something that they know they want. The more difficult you can make leaving, the less customer churn you'll see in your programs.

RECESSION PROOF

THE CLOSING OF PART 1
The Connected Economy.

RECESSION PROOF

PART 1 – CUSTOMER OBSESSION

Back in the late 90's and early 2000's, the global economy underwent a radical change that caught many businesses off guard. The internet, and more specifically, connected personal devices, advanced rapidly and changed the way that businesses interacted with their customers. In short, markets went from service based (the service economy) to digital based (the digital economy).

No, that doesn't mean that *services* disappeared… just that businesses had to shift from being service and relationship based to being digitally based.

Probably the best example of this shift was the travel agent business. If you are old enough to remember travelling in the 80s and 90s, then you might just remember travel agents – the specialists who knew about all the best travel experiences and properties around the world.

They were the go-to people whenever one wanted to go on a vacation or even just book a flight. You'd tell them where you wanted to go and then they'd head out to do all the research for you, negotiate the best prices, and make sure that everything, and everyone, was all set up to have the best travel experience possible.

If there was an issue that popped up, they took care of it. If your flight got changed unexpectedly, they took care of it. Many times, if you needed someone to swing by your vacant home while away, they'd take care of it for you. Their job was to take care of all things travel for you, and they were quite good at it… until the digital economy came around.

Almost overnight, the travel agent industry was decimated by newfangled internet-based business models like Expedia, Priceline, Hotwire, and a range of others. These new "kids" on the block swooped in and offered consumers *instant* access to type in a destination of interest in a web browser and then see lists of options, complete with pictures, descriptions, reviews, excursions, and, best of all, cheap prices.

The travel agents of old didn't stand a chance. I mean, why would a consumer drive down to the travel agent's office, tell them about where they want to go, look through a stack of brochures, and then pay for their travel *plus* the agent's commission when they could just head on over to their new favorite ".com" site and have a trip selected and booked in an instant… and for cheaper!?!

But it wasn't just the travel industry where this was happening. Real estate, automotive, consumer products, and pretty much every other industry and vertical were all shaken and stirred with the advent of the digital economy.

During this time, consumers enjoyed fast access to information and could know everything there was to know about a product or service in a matter of minutes. They could know what was offered, features and benefits (and drawbacks), how others felt about the company offering it, other companies offering the same or similar goods and services, what kind of social good each of those companies were involved in (or scandals), and could even compare pricing against the various competitors to ensure that they were getting the best deal.

As you can imagine, or remember, the wave of the digital economy in the 90s and 2000s created immense competitive pressures for the vast majority of businesses. What was once a friendly marketplace became extremely cutthroat. Customers were in control and most businesses didn't know how to react.

Companies across the board were forced to lower prices and cut services/support in order to meet the demands of the new economy – the "cheap" economy.

The men and women in the middle – like the travel agents – were no longer necessary. The services, support, and perks that they offered couldn't compete with the cut rate prices and easy access to information being offered on the internet. People were no longer willing to pay a premium for "service"… it was all about price.

Consumers became obsessed with good deals and had the power at their fingertips to find them, so they did. This era of "cheap" created *massive* winners and losers in the global economy as margins shrunk to a sliver and *sales volume* became the objective of businesses everywhere.

Businesses had to sell a whole heck of a lot of products and services in order to make a living. The problem was, most small businesses hadn't been set up on a volume-based model, they were service-based. As a result, Ma, Pa, and many other small businesses around the world were gobbled up by the .com behemoths who were more efficient and could sell for cheaper – who could sell and deliver on small margins at a high volume.

Fast forward now to the 2020's, and the digital economy still rules the roost... but things are changing. For all of the *convenience* and *low cost* that the digital economy provided for consumers and business buyers over the last couple of decades, it hasn't given people what they *really* wanted. I mean, sure, they got whatever it is that they paid for, but it turns out that **what they paid for wasn't enough**. An unfulfilled need remained after almost every purchase.

As one might imagine, the "cheap" economy had its downsides. Low prices led many, if not most, businesses to cut corners... to lower the quality of their products/services... to deny adequate support to customers who had questions... and to make anything that isn't buying from them difficult.

Now, after a couple of decades of this, **people are fed up.**

The realization that "cheap" leads to an abysmal experience has left markets yearning for quality, for service, and for the feeling of connection that they had back in the 90s and 2000s. Put more simply, people realized that they want the ease of the digital economy with the *connection* of the service economy. They want the best of both worlds, and they are willing to pay higher prices for it.

In The "Connected" Economy, Consumers Want Both Digital Connection & Relational Connection.

If you've ever wondered where the heck "influencers" came from, and why they became a thing, this is it. Influencers offer *relational* connection in a digital world. They are the bridge between what people have wanted over the last decade and what businesses have delivered.

Let's be clear, though – this section closing is not about influencers. They are merely an example used to illustrate what people want and how they've found a way to get it in the absence of businesses offering it. That said, the intent of this chapter – from the customer knowing the owner, to the customer's experience, to the customer's membership – is to highlight how you as a business owner can give people what they want, connection.

When done correctly, <u>a business' obsession with its customers should lead to its customers' obsession with the business</u>. It's a two-way street, and it's important to remember that. Obsession, from a business sense, stems from a desire to want the best for another while expecting the same in return.

As a business owner, it is in your best interest to foster these types of relationships (because that's what they are) with the customers that patronize your business. When you lead, they will follow, and resiliency in your business will result.

PART 2

An Obsession With Serving A Growing Number Of Customers

RECESSION PROOF

Having worked with many hundreds of business owners over the years, I can attest that most all of them shared one common trait – they LOVED getting a new customer. And for good reason. The most exciting thing in almost any business is the thrill of having a brand new customer ring your cash register or ding your payment processing system.

The joy felt in the moment of acquiring a new customer is unlike anything else; kinda like a positive reinforcement system reminding you that you're doing something right.

Unfortunately, though, for as much as most entrepreneurs love the feeling of acquiring a new customer, **there are surprisingly few who can call themselves *obsessed* with getting more of them**.

I know that statement might seem a bit out of place. The vast majority of entrepreneurs love new customers and spend their days, nights, and weekends dreaming about how they'll get more of them. I'm not questioning their *desire* to have more new customers in the slightest.

Instead, I'm calling out the fact that most entrepreneurs are in love with the *idea* of new customers... but aren't in love with the processes that will attract more of them to their business.

Case in point, few entrepreneurs are _so_ obsessed with serving more customers that they are willing to cold call prospects. Likewise, few entrepreneurs lie awake at night (on a consistent basis) mapping out the campaigns and split tests they'll run in their marketing. Even fewer compulsively study marketing and sales and then routinely *implement* what they learn.

More often than not, entrepreneurs *dream* about a growing business without giving enough attention to the strategies and tactics that will bring new customers in. Instead, they dream about the shortcuts and shiny objects... and obsess over the end result _instead of the process_.

That's all well and fine, but, in my experience...

> # A Business Does Not Grow To Its Potential Until They Have An Absolute Obsession With <u>The Process</u> That Brings Them New Customers.

That is what it means to be obsessed with serving a growing number of customers. When you love the process, you get to enjoy the result.

This is especially true during down economies when first transactions with new customers can become harder and harder to come by. People are typically making less money and, as a result, spending less as well. The money that they _do_ spend is spent cautiously; with high skepticism and higher frugality.

Recessions are no time for a business to mess around with haphazard customer acquisition processes. <u>Businesses need to be laser focused on knowing exactly what inputs drive results</u>. Once they know that, then they must fervently do those things so that they keep a steady flow of new customers into their business. That's the obsession they need to have.

But how exactly can you know what _inputs_ drive results so that you can focus on, and obsess over, them?

THE CONCEPT

When looking at acquiring new customers, it's important that you keep things as simple as you possibly can. There are many, many, strategies and tactics out there that you can quickly get lost in. Some are good, some are bad, but most are just confusing.

That's why, in this book, we're going to focus on the most basic fundamentals of marketing and sales... because, if being honest with you, **most business owners are 100% clueless when it comes to**

the fundamentals. Yet, the fundamentals are the key to profitable business, especially during a recession.

I don't mean the above statement about business owners being clueless in a derogatory way by any means. The truth of it is that, in today's day and age, business owners are bombarded with so much information about marketing and sales that the core fundamentals are lost. It's become so bad in recent years that even many university business degree graduates, including MBAs, know next to nothing about marketing and sales fundamentals.

Again, not their fault. Their knowledge is a direct reflection of what they were taught, and what they were taught, in most cases, was not necessarily wrong... it just omitted the fundamentals.

So, let's start at the basics.

At the root of every business lies three often unanswered questions:

---

1)Are my customers looking for my business?

2)Am I looking for my customers?

3)Do my customers find my business by happenstance?

Knowing the answers to these questions is essential to knowing how you should approach your market, as each is going to influence your strategy. A business who has customers looking *for* them is going to have a vastly different marketing and sales strategy than a business whose customers find them by happenstance. Likewise for businesses who need to go out and find their customers.

To keep the idea here very simple, and to prevent over-emphasizing on the topic, I'll sum this up in 3 short bullet points:

- If your customers are actively looking for your business then your strategy will revolve around making it as easy as possible for them to find you (e.g. having updated map listings in Google Maps, Apple Maps, Bing Maps, etc., having easy to reach physical locations, and/or having strong search engine optimization).
- If you are looking for your customers then your strategy will be centered around how you find, target, and attract those customers as cost effectively as possible.
- If your customers find you by happenstance then your strategy should be to change your business model as quickly as possible… as businesses that are reliant on happenstance are typically the first to go under during a recession.

Naturally, having a business where customers actively seek you out is the ultimate goal. I mean, who wouldn't want to sit back and see sales coming in without having to advertise or market, right?

But that's not the reality for most businesses. While they may have *some* new customers who seek out their business because of word of mouth or referrals, it's not the norm. The vast majority of their new customers come to them either because they marketed to them, or the person found them by mere happenstance. More often than not, it's the case of happenstance that brings the customer to their business. The person just happened to be driving by, or they were at the business next door and decided to pop over, or they randomly just stumbled upon the business some other way. There was no specific activity performed by the business that could be attributed to bringing them in… they just kind of showed up.

Here's the thing, though, happenstance, and even being sought out by customers, are <u>not forms of new customer acquisition that a business can rely on</u>. No person can ever forecast how many referrals they'll get, how many searches they'll have, or how many people will randomly show up ready to buy. Those things just kind of happen, like a little bonus for the business owner.

That's why, when we look at how you obtain new customers, neither of these "strategies" should be focused on. Sure, customer referrals, searches, and word of mouth are all great things… but you'll earn those by being obsessed with your customers and their experience (part 1 of this book). <u>The more important thing for you to focus on as it relates to customer acquisition will be how you find, target, and attract your customers as cost effectively as possible</u>.

While making your business easier to find for customers looking for you is a good thing to do, it cannot be considered a strategy. Why? Because, when people are looking for your business, you are dependent on factors that you cannot control. If all you are doing for customer acquisition is making your business easier to find then you are at the mercy of market demand. As market demand goes up and down, so does your business.

<u>The key component in any strategy is that you have some mechanism of control</u>. That's what makes it a strategy. If you have no control over the battlefield of business, then you have no strategy.

All that said, and the reason I point this out, is because while it is good to make your business easier to find, it cannot be your only means of acquiring new customers. **<u>In every business, there comes a time when, such as in a recession, you have actively go out to find your customers if you want to have any hope of surviving.</u>**

That means that you have to have a strategy and plan for how you will go-to-market.

RECESSION PROOF

PART 2, SECTION 1
The Go-To-Market Strategy

RECESSION PROOF

THE STRATEGY

Everybody has heard of one, few know what one really is, and fewer yet have implemented one. The Go-To-Market (GTM) Strategy is an often overlooked and under-utilized tool available to small businesses.

Historically, though, the GTM strategy has been something used by "big" business and not by everyday entrepreneurs and small businesses. Often times, small business owners look at it as not much more than a 50-page report about market demographics that an overpriced consultant puts together. Useless folly that will sit on a shelf for years until it is dusted off... and thrown away.

"A failure to plan is a plan to fail". Variations of this quote have been around for more than a century, yet the message still rings true today. Applied to the topic of business, if you don't have a plan for how you will go out to your market to find customers – a GTM strategy – then you might as well plan to fail.

Fortunately, though, you don't need to assemble some 50-page report that ends up sitting on a shelf for a few years. That would just be a waste. Instead, an option available to you is a "lite" GTM strategy; a plan that outlines how you'll go out to find and acquire customers without all the useless fluff.

At its core, a lite GTM strategy is simply a plan for how you will:

1. Identify who your desired customer really is (the ones you prefer to work with).
2. Figure out where they can be found.
3. Determine how you'll make contact with them in the locations where they can be found.
4. Understand what will motivate them to buy (e.g. pain points, drivers, etc.).
5. Make them an initial offer that will pull them into your sales process
6. Ascend them into a continuity program.

That's it. Just 6 quick bullet points that encompasses everything needed for a decent GTM strategy. It really doesn't need to be any more complex than that. Just 6 questions answered on a single piece of paper that drives the overarching components of your business' strategy. The shorter and more to the point it is, the better.

To provide a few examples of this, below are GTM strategies that will help give you a frame of reference for what different types of businesses might do…

CONSULTING BUSINESSES

Who is the desired customer: Small business owners who have budget to, and actively are, advertising (as one example).

Where they can be found: Identify them through ads they run. Find their contact information from their website or from state business filings (public record).

How contact will be made with them: Mail them a series of compelling direct-mail sales letters that entice them to raise their hand as a prospect who wants to learn how to get better advertising results.

What will motivate them to buy:

- Homing in on the less than desired results they are currently getting.
- Hinting that they might be missing something that is the key to better results, thereby creating curiosity.
- Offering stats and testimonials showing social proof of the consulting firm's results.

What offer is made to them: Typically a book as the low-ticket, low-resistance, front end, with immediate upsell of an in-person workshop as the mid-ticket profit generator.

How to get them to join a continuity program: At the end of the workshop, offer them an annual done-with-you coaching package.

ENTERPRISE SOFTWARE COMPANY (GENERIC)

Who is the desired customer: Decision makers within mid to large businesses.

Where they can be found: LinkedIn, industry association rosters, trade shows, and list marketplaces.

How contact will be made with them: Cold calling, direct mail marketing, industry trade show booths, training webinars, & white paper downloads.

What will motivate them to buy: Inefficient business processes & performance improvement pressure from leadership.

What offer is made to them: Free demo or trial access.

How to get them to join a continuity program: Offer a subscription after the demo or trial access. Have a salesperson convince them of the benefits.

HEALTH CARE SYSTEMS (HOSPITALS & CLINICS)

Who is the desired customer: Every insured person in a geographic region. Typically, middle class families who are okay with generic care (compared to top-notch care).

Where they can be found: Nearby to middle class neighborhood grocery stores and pharmacies (as the central "hub" of the neighborhood).

How contact will be made with them: Prominent corner location Urgent Care that is nearby to the grocery store or pharmacy. Also, monthly print mail is sent out to households within the vicinity informing them of the clinic's location and urgent care services.

What will motivate them to buy: Non-life threatening medical concerns that naturally occur through everyday life.

What offer is made to them: Quick access to medical professionals who can help diagnose, alleviate, or treat symptoms.

<u>How to get them to join a continuity program</u>: At the end of the visit, schedule a follow up appointment with an in-network primary care clinic or specialist as a means to capture their long-term business.

Of course, depending on your type of business, your GTM strategy might vary drastically from what is outlined here. That's okay, as it should be custom tailored for your business and what makes sense in your market. There are, however, a few rules that you should follow when creating your GTM strategy:

GO-TO-MARKET RULES:

Rule #1: Don't Think You Can Get Away Without Marketing

It almost never fails. Times get tough, revenue begins to slow, and one of the first things that a business cuts budget on is marketing.

I don't know what it is about entrepreneurs that leads them to believe that the best thing to do for their business is to turn off their marketing so that they can "save" money for more important things. It's a trait that seems to be engrained in the psyche, though.

But here's the truth: *very few* businesses survive for long without marketing.

That's because marketing is to business like food is to a person. Sure, you can last a short while without it, but eventually you're going to need it if you want to survive.

Rule #2: Don't Be A Marketing "Victim" To Vultures

Under the *traditional* model, most marketing fails more than it succeeds. That's just a truth.

Businesses head out on a mission fueled by the belief that the marketing they will do will be a wild success and they will be living on Easy Street in almost no time at all.

Ask almost any business owner or leader how well they think their upcoming campaign will perform and they'll answer optimistically. In fact, the optimistic answer that they tell you isn't even the truth – they are MORE optimistic than they are willing to say aloud. What they are actually thinking… or dreaming… is that this next campaign will be the ticket that they need.

In most cases, it's an idealistic view disconnected from reality.

"The Typical Entrepreneur And Business Owner Is Essentially Clueless When It Comes To Advertising And Marketing."

Dan Kennedy

The average entrepreneur tends to look at what all the big companies in their industry do for marketing and think that they should model it. Just like the big brands, they do sponsorships, direct mail coupon books and generic postcards, "brand-building" social media ads, billboards, and a whole range of other silly, silly, things.

I say "silly" things because not one of these things is likely to give them a healthy return on investment. It's just broad-based advertising where 99+% of the money spent is wasted on people who are not, and likely never will be, customers of the business.

The business owners simply don't know any better.

This makes them prime targets for all types of business _vultures_. Also known as _many (but not all)_ digital marketers, advertising agencies, branding consultants, and all these other folk who promise them results but have NO WAY to meaningfully track performance as it relates to dollars and cents in bank accounts. Instead, they track views, likes, reach, shares, and a whole bunch of other nonsense. Last time I checked, I can't cash any of these things at the bank. Nor can I cash the often presented "brand presence".

Yet, marketing "consultants" of all shapes and sizes push these near useless metrics in front of entrepreneurs and business owners all the time. It's their way of showcasing what they construe as *value* when the dollars and cents of their work doesn't add up to true ROI.

They say things like:

"It's all a part of the process"

"You have to wait until your brand is more established… then you'll see the real returns"

"The amount of shares and likes that your ad got indicates that you're on the right track"

"This was some great branding for your business"

Have you ever heard these sayings (or something similar) from someone you've been working with for marketing? If yes, I'll let you in on a little secret – **it's all bullshit**. They're either *willfully* covering up their lack of performance by throwing a shade of positivity over it, or they are honestly ignorant to what real results look like and shouldn't be in the profession they are.

Sure, the things they told you aren't *technically* bad. Getting your business more exposure in the market never hurts… but if you're pulling out Jacksons and Benjamins (cash, for those non-Americans) to pay for advertising and marketing then you'd best be getting them back, plus more. Your profitability depends on it.

That said, it is absolutely imperative that you identify what good marketing looks like and sear it into your mind. That way, when you see and/or hear the garbage that will inevitably be pitched, you can call bullshit where and when you see it.

Rule #3: Don't <u>Ever</u> Expect That You'll Get It Right The First Time

In golf, a hole-in-one is rare. It's a feat reserved for great players who have worked hard to hone their skills… and have gotten lucky on one shot out of thousands. <u>Marketing, especially advertising, is absolutely no different</u>.

An entrepreneur can study marketing for decades before running an advertisement or campaign and still never get the proverbial hole-in-one, home run, or touchdown on their campaigns. The ball might only get halfway to the hole many times; still requiring a few swings to sink the shot.

Unfortunately, though, many entrepreneurs give up playing before they ever make the hole. Or, they *have* hit a hole-in-one before and expect to do so again and again on every shot they take from there forward. As a result, when they have to take two, three, or even four shots on a given campaign, they end up hopping off the greens and heading home in frustration.

The problem here is *expectation*. They expect success and then find frustration when they don't achieve it right away. Well, if you were to ask any successful marketer what it took to become successful, they'd tell you that you have to <u>expect a mediocre first shot and then split test your way to success from there</u>. If you get surprised by a hole in one every now and then, great, but it shouldn't be the expectation. Split testing your way to a great campaign is the more likely path.

Rule #4: Make It Personal

In today's day and age – the age of the internet – many have lost their way. Mass media has diluted our collective expectations of, and for, human interaction. As a result, so few businesses communicate with their prospects and customers on a personal basis that when one does it becomes an immediate and clear differentiator.

For this reason, and many more, you should look at your GTM strategy through the lens of how you can make every contact with a prospect as specific and personal to them as you possibly can. The more that you can get your prospect to think "This is exactly for me!" when they read your letter or see your ad, the better.

That's why I'm a huge advocate of marketing on a named prospect basis for most small businesses. Yes, that means knowing the actual names of everyone you market to. Strange as it may sound, this is what will set your business apart from the crowd.

PART 2, SECTION 2
Marketing Assets, Not Activity

RECESSION PROOF

THE STRATEGY

Once you've defined your GTM strategy, it'll be time for you to actually go out to the market. No business exists inside a vacuum, and in order to find and acquire new customers you are going to have to put your business out there. That means marketing. More specifically, it means that you're going to need marketing *assets* that help you to consistently and reliably reach your ideal prospects.

As was covered in the preface to this book, traditional mass marketing doesn't work well during recessions. It takes up too much time and costs too much money only to get your business somewhat random exposure to people who potentially, just maybe, might have an interest in your products or services.

Most businesses today practice marketing as a verb – they make a lot of noise in their market with mass marketing like billboards on the side of the road, broadly targeted mailers in the mailbox, "premium" physical locations, social media posts and ads galore, and all the rest. They put a lot of effort into creating a "presence" so that they might randomly capture the attention of people who potentially might have interest in their product or service.

Don't get me wrong, I don't have a problem with any of these things *as marketing channels*. I love the specificity and impact of targeted mail, I adore the benefits of a prime physical location, and I enjoy the reach and cost effectiveness of social media. What I *don't* like is the marketing strategy that is most often employed within these channels.

Essentially, what most businesses do is use these marketing channels to scream "*We EXIST! Here we are!*" as many times as they can so that *random* people might notice them. They make a lot of noise… but don't actually offer the people on the other end of their message any value or incentive to take action. Nor do they do a very good job at targeting their messages. The hope is simply that enough random people take note about the fact that they exist that, one day in the future, a few of them might give their business a try and become a customer. The visual representation of this might look something like this…

> **Lots of Noise → Random Attention → Knowledge of Existence → Sporadic Sales**

While this approach might work in times of plenty during good economies it can become problematic in down trending economies. The problem is that as market conditions sour and there are fewer and fewer buyers in a given market, there are more and more businesses who are screaming – often more desperately – for their attention.

The reality of the situation is that as markets deteriorate during a recession, consumers as a whole spend less, thereby making the pool of buyers for any specific product or service a shrinking entity. Competition for those buyers heats up and it becomes increasingly difficult for individual businesses to stand out. So, what most businesses do is stand up and make more noise than they used to. Businesses who previously made next to no noise all of a sudden pipe up, and businesses who were previously making noise pipe up louder.

As you can imagine, the marketplace quickly gets noisy, and customers, even more quickly, tune it all out.

What worked during times of plenty begins to no longer work. The strategy of having massive marketing action – and making lots of "noise" – quickly becomes a waste of time. A new strategy is needed in order to keep a steady flow of customers coming in the door with cash in hand. One that will work _despite_ the noise of what everyone else is doing.

This is where asset-based marketing strategies will come in handy… for the businesses that know how to implement them that is.

THE TACTICS:

Asset Based Marketing

To revisit the notion that marketing, done correctly, is not something that you do… but something that you OWN., the cornerstone of a good GTM strategy is having a marketing asset that you can deploy.

What this means is that your marketing should **not** just be an activity. It should be a *thing*; a thing that you point to and say "that's how I market my business right there". It should be like a self-inflating raft that - no matter what pool of customers you deploy it in, it looks the same, performs the same, and delivers the same results. It's reliable and repeatable, and there is no mystery around how it works.

Yes, it might have multiple components, and, over time, you might change it so that it looks slightly different… but, at its core, it's all the same. It's a tool that you can repeatably deploy in different pools of customers in order to reliably pull them into your business.

When you have this type of marketing asset, you no longer need to make a lot of noise like everyone else in your industry and market do. You can sit back and (mostly) relax as your asset brings customers into your business. This then allows you to focus more time on being obsessed with your customer's outcome, as that will drive retention, increase sales volume, and improve the chance of referrals.

So, what does a marketing asset look like, and how do you build one?

Well, it all starts with a few core concepts…

Everything Boils Down To The List

When working with a new client, two of the first questions that I ask are 1)Where is your list of customers and leads?, and 2)What mechanisms do you have in place that feeds new names into this list?

A business owner's response to these questions typically tells me everything that I need to know about the level of marketing that they are doing. If they have a list that includes both customers and prospects _and_ can show me what mechanisms feed that list then I know that they are fairly advanced marketers, or can become advanced fairly quickly. If, however, they don't have a list, or have a list but can't showcase the mechanisms, then I know we've got some work to do.

Before we get too deep into this concept, though, it'll be important to understand **why** "the list" is so important.

When marketing and selling in your business, you have the option of targeting:

1. People who are not in your list (the masses)
2. People who are in your list but haven't purchased yet (leads)
3. People in your list who have purchased recently (customers)
4. People in your list who purchased a long time ago (dormant or lost customers)

Naturally, the people in #2 (leads) and #3 (customers) will have the highest conversion rates by far. This should just be common sense to any business owner. The person who has given you either their contact information (leads) or who have paid you (customers) have already identified themselves as people who are in the market for what you do and will convert the best.

The fact that they have identified themselves as _in your market_ is _very_ important.

I don't know about you, but if I'm going to sell something, I don't want to stand on the corner screaming at the top of my lungs out to the masses saying "Hey you over there! Come buy from me!". That's just a terrible strategy. Even if I've "targeted" the masses that I'm shouting to, I still have no idea which ones of them are actually in the market for what I sell. I'm just making a lot of noise in hopes that somebody, anybody, will buy.

As was covered earlier in this book, this is how most businesses advertise. No offense to you if you're one of them, but as the economy tightens up, this will be a fool's strategy.

That's because…

You Should Only Sell To People Who Have Already Pre-Identified Themselves As Someone In The Market For What You Do.

That means that they have done something that has gotten their name on your list. Let's reiterate this, because it is important: <u>they have done *something*, via some form of action, to get themselves on your list</u>.

If they haven't taken an action that landed them on your list then you should not sell to them. They're not yet worthy of your sales effort. And, if they *have* done something to get themselves on your list, then you should be making them offers on a routine basis so that you maximize sales and serve them at the highest level.

The hard truth of the world is that sales effort costs money. It costs real dollars and cents to get your business in front of the right people so that you can convince them that your product or service is the best for them at that moment in time given their circumstances. That's why the list is so important.

The list is <u>the one thing</u> – the one *asset* – in your business that allows you to cost effectively sell to the right people at the right time. If you have a healthy list, you will have a healthy business… in any economy.

The Mechanism That Builds Your List

Now that we've covered "why" the list is so important, let's hit the reverse button and back up to the mechanism you use to build your list. This is your tool that helps you to attract people who are interested in what you offer and then screens them for the characteristics of your ideal customer.

Note how the tool that builds your list should have a screening mechanism that filters out the potentially bad customers and attracts the right ones. You don't want to waste your time and selling effort chasing customers who won't be your best, so it makes sense to filter for them right from the start.

Many businesses get this wrong and head out into the market to try and build the biggest list that they can. It ends up costing them a lot of money, and results only in a bloated, unhealthy, list.

What they often don't realize is that...

> ### Selling To An Unhealthy List Is Almost As Bad As Selling To The Masses.

Selling to an unhealthy list wastes effort and money that could otherwise be spent on better prospects and/or processes within your business. That said, it's better to have a small healthy list than it is to have a big and unhealthy one. After all, when looked at with an honest grain of salt, most small businesses should only need a relatively small and manageable list that is paired with a customer obsession in order to thrive.

Now, let's get back to how you *build* that list.

When creating the mechanism for building your list, you have a handful of components that will all come together like cogs in a machine. This machine, put in the most simple of words, is your advertising vehicle.

But don't get caught up in the word of advertising. A lot of people today associate advertising with just social media ads. While that can certainly be *one* way that you advertise, it is by no means the whole enchilada. The way I look at it, depending on your business structure, advertising can be your content marketing, your cold-calling, your direct-mail, and almost any other activity you do that allows you to be made visible to new customers in your chosen market(s). If you're doing anything to make your business visible to your target market then, at least for the purposes of this book, that can be considered your advertising.

That said, let's break down your advertising vehicle into the four components that will all come together to make your advertising successful at bringing in new customers.

1) THE TARGETING COMPONENT

As you can imagine, any time you are going to spend money or effort to advertise, it simply makes the most sense to focus your efforts on the sections of "the masses" that are most likely to have your best customers in them. In social media advertising, they coined this "targeting". The platforms allow advertisers to "target" their ad delivery to users who had certain interests and traits. In direct-mail advertising, they called it "list refinement"; where advertisers segment their mailing list based on certain characteristics of the recipients. In sales, they termed it "prospecting"; where salespeople manually research targets before performing outreach activity.

Whatever it is that you call it is up to you. The more important thing is that you don't skip over it. Targeting is a very important part of the equation in new customer acquisition and shouldn't be ignored.

The reason that it's so important is because, when advertising, you want to get the right message in front of the right people so that it "lands" with them. An absolutely phenomenal sales message that would otherwise be a multimillion-dollar driver in your business can end up falling flat on its face *IF* put in front of the wrong eyes.

Conversely, a crummy sales message put in front of the *right* eyes can be the driver of a healthy list and overall sales process. The "who" that sees your marketing message is more important as the "what" that your message conveys.

Naturally, you should always want to have the best sales message put in front of the best people for that message, as a good message-to-market match will ensure the most cost-effective utilization of marketing spend. But before we get too far ahead of ourselves talking about the message that you send in your advertising, let's cover what good and bad targeting looks like:

- Running an ad for weightlifting apparel to an audience mostly made up of little old grannies is probably not the best targeting match.
- Running an ad for dental marketing services in a dental trade magazine is typically a good targeting match.
- Sending postcard mailers to massive swaths of neighborhoods offering a smoking deal on a new furnace or AC system, believe it or not, is *not* the best targeting match. (Not *everyone* who lives in a home is going to be a good match for this offer)
- Sending a printed letter inviting someone who just moved into a new home to come try your nearby restaurant is typically a good targeting match.
- Renting a billboard on a busy street for a jewelry store 6 blocks away is not a good targeting match.
- Paying a well-known person in a given market (an influencer) to send a promotional email for a relevant product to their followers is a good targeting match.

There are a million more examples that we could cover, but, hopefully, you're starting to see a trend of what constitutes putting the right message in front of the right person… and what doesn't. In a nutshell, good targeting all boils down to knowing <u>who it is you're going after</u> and then identifying <u>the media that will allow you to get your message in front of the most of those people</u>, without putting your message in front of too many people who don't match your target characteristics.

In order to do that, though, you'll need to start by identifying, very specifically, **who** you are going to deliver your sales message to.

What are their traits? Where do they live? How much money do they make? Are they married? Have kids? Have a thriving business in a specific industry? Etc…

You don't have to get too crazy in level of detail here, although you can. The important thing is that you identify what the *core* traits of your best customers are so that when you go to choose a media you can select one that you have confidence will put your message in front of the right people. Once you do that, it'll be time for the fun part – how you actually get your message in front of them.

When looking to find where your ideal clients are so that you can most cost-effectively deliver your sales message, you have a few options:

1. You can <u>rent advertising space in *content* streams</u> where people meeting certain traits tend to give their attention. This includes social media, magazines, radio channels, e-commerce sites, blog sites, game channels, video-streaming platforms, and other streams that entertain or educate people through content.

2. You can <u>buy mailing/contact lists from list brokers</u> who compile massive lists of consumer and business contacts and then identify certain characteristics of them. For example, if you wanted to, you could buy mailing lists focused on select neighborhoods in Boise, Idaho that only includes 35-40 year old mothers who own their own home, are members of the Republican party, and have a birthday in May.

3. You can <u>rent promotional placement from influencers in your market</u> who already have the eyes, ears, and trust of the people matching your ideal customer profile.

4. You can <u>create your own content channel that attracts your ideal customer profile</u> to you so that you can then drip your sales message to them (e.g. a blog, YouTube channel, email subscriber list, etc.).

5. You can <u>research your market and find contact information yourself</u>, as most all consumer and business information is available in some public format.

There's no right or wrong answer as to which of these options you choose, as each has its benefits and drawbacks. In many cases, it'll be best to dip your toes in the waters of each to see where you get the best results based on your targeting.

2)A LEAD MAGNET

Whenever advertising, the second most important thing after targeting is having a low-resistance offer that, when put in front of the right person, is an absolute no-brainer for them. Something that aligns to what they want and need so perfectly, and with so little risk for them, that they simply can't refuse.

This is what is called a Lead Magnet. It's a "magnetically" attractive offer that pulls the right customer in so that you can capture them as a lead and *then* sell more to them. In retail, they call it the "Loss Leader"; the product that the company is willing to take a loss on at the front end of the sales cycle so that they can get the customer in the door and then upsell them on other products and services.

The concept is the same between Lead Magnet and Loss Leader, but I tend to prefer the term Lead Magnet. This is because I believe that you don't always have to take a monetary loss in order to capture new leads and customers, which Loss Leader implies. Taking a slight loss on customer acquisition is quite normal but having a breakeven, or even profitable, front end should always be the goal.

But let's stop right here for a moment and take an aside. If you're like most business owners, then you might be thinking to yourself "why in the world would I spend money on advertising if I'm not going to make it right back immediately, and then some?"

That's a fair question, and one that I come across all the time. My answer is always the same...

The Goal Of Advertising Is To Gain High-Quality Leads, Not Sales.

I know that this might seem a bit backwards but hear me out. If you're doing things right in your business by having a customer obsession, then <u>a high-quality lead is worth more than just a sale</u>.

One of the biggest mistakes that I see businesses repeatedly make is advertising for the sole purpose of making money. They want a sale, so they focus their marketing around getting just that, and they do.

The thing is… this is *extremely* shortsighted.

When you advertise with the objective of gaining sales, you will get a *handful* of people who will take you up on your offer. That's certainly a good thing, but like the old iceberg analogy where only a small section is visible above the water line, the approach is missing the bigger chunk below.

To be more specific, when you advertise for the purpose of gaining sales, you often have many perfectly good prospects who pass you up because they were *interested* but not quite ready yet. Maybe they needed more information. Maybe they needed to feel like they know your business a bit better. Maybe they were busy at the time and didn't have time to pull out their card. There could be a hundred reasons why they pass on the offer, but the fact of the matter is that many of them do, and will, pass you by when you advertise for the purpose of sales.

These are all people <u>lost to your business</u> that *should* have been added to your list so that you could sell to them over time. You spent money to get your ad in front of them, and they didn't bite because the ad was too quick to try and sell to them.

Advertising will forever feel "expensive" if this is happening in your business. Money is spent to gain exposure to the right people, but the majority of those people simply look and move on, never to be heard from again. That makes your cost per lead shoot up while also limiting your potential growth. This is especially true when we're in the midst of a recession and people are more skeptical of how they spend their money (more people want more information before making a final purchasing decision).

That brings us back to "the list". People who are on the list can purchase on their own timeline. Of course, you'll do your best to influence that timeline with some urgency and scarcity in your offers… but the list is the tool in your toolbelt that allows you to sell to these interested parties *over time* instead of in an instance.

Remember, if you have a healthy list, you will have a healthy business… in any economy.

That's why a lead magnet is so important. It's designed to capture the iceberg of people who would otherwise pass by your business if you tried to sell what it is you do to them right away. It is the tool that you can use to capture as many high-quality leads as possible in every targeted distribution channel you place it in.

Using this book as an example, I never once made the offer of buying the physical book as my front-end lead magnet unless it was packaged as a part of an insane offer. The price of the book by itself, while completely reasonable in my eyes, would be a deterrent to capturing leads, and, therefore, would hamper my list building goals. Of course, my *ultimate* goal was to sell the book… but I couldn't lead my advertising with that offer. So, I instead led with lower resistance offers that I knew my leads would say "yes" to. These were freebie offers, or $3 frameworks, or low-cost virtual workshops, or other low barrier to entry offers that allowed me to capture as many high-quality leads as possible.

In my case, I used multiple lead magnets, but that doesn't mean that just one wouldn't have been enough. Depending on your business, a single lead magnet might the sole driver of new leads or a handful of lead magnets might be. There's no right or wrong answer to how many you use so long as you are using them and can manage the scale of management and fulfillment with them.

As you can likely imagine, part of the goal with the lead magnet is to gain the person's contact information (if you don't already have it). This allows you to keep in contact with them over time, and preferably through different media (email, print mail, text, video, etc.), so that you can indoctrinate them into your business and sell to them over time *without* having to run another ad.

The second part of the goal for your lead magnet is simply to get your leads to bite the hook that you've put out into the marketplace with your advertising. This is because, for one reason or another, human psychology has evolved in such a way that people don't typically like to make big decisions all at once. BUT, if a decision is broken down into smaller, seemingly less risky, decisions then they are more likely to say "yes" to each subsequent decision after the first.

There is a documentary on Netflix, The Push, that illustrates this to the extreme. In the show, a normal everyday guy is, unknowingly, placed into a staged scenario where he is forced to make one difficult decision after the other in an effort to save himself from potential incrimination. The premise of the show is to see how far they can get someone to go into committing a crime by leading them to make incremental decisions that escalate from benign to extreme. Essentially, they want to see if they can get the guy – who is in every way normal – to commit murder by pushing a guy off a ledge. I won't spoil the outcome of the show but will say that you'd be surprised by how far they get this guy to go simply by leading him from one decision to the next.

The power of incremental decisions is enormous. When a person might see a decision as being big and "scary", they have a very low chance of saying "yes" to it. This is true whether they are making big life-impacting choices or simple buying decisions. The bigger that they *perceive* the decision to be, the less likely they will be to say "yes" to it.

Conversely, if a person has the option of sequentially making less scary decisions – even if they know those decisions lead to the same outcome as the big decision – then they are more likely to say "yes". The risk is lower, so they are more inclined to give it a try. And, once they say "yes" to the first decision, they are more inclined to say "yes" to any subsequent decisions after that if they got what they expected (or more) from the first one. That means that by saying "yes" to your lead magnet your leads are naturally more apt to say "yes" to a second offer that you make… and that leads us to the Sales Funnel.

3)THE SALES FUNNEL

Unlike the lead magnet where the goal was just to get leads to say "yes", the Sales Funnel is where you get to sell what you actually want to sell. It's also where you make your profits.

Before we get too deep into sales funnels, though, it'll be important to define what they are, as there are different meanings in different circles. For example, in the digital marketing circle, a sales funnel is a sales driven landing page with upsell processes for maximizing average cart value. Conversely, in the professional sales circle, a sales funnel is the full customer journey from initial brand discovery through to purchase, often broken down into phases and counted by how many prospects or opportunities a salesperson has in each phase.

While not wrong, neither of these definitions are what we'll use for this book. Instead, **we'll define Sales Funnel as the _process_ that you use to convert a lead into a long term or high value customer**.

This process might be online, it might be offline, or it might be a combo of the two. It might be short, it might be long, or it might be in the middle. It might include hard sell tactics, or it might include soft sell tactics. All of these variables, and more, are things that are fully dependent on what it is that you are selling and who you are selling to.

What really matters is that you have a process, and repeatedly point leads and customers to the appropriate point in that process so that they progress forwards and ascend in value and loyalty for your business. This is how you maximize sales, and…

Maximizing Sales Is The Goal Of A Sales Funnel.

PART 2 – GROWTH OBSESSION

Whether you have a single step sales funnel with one core offer or a fifty step sales funnel with many offers made in ascending order will again depend on your business. For the sake of this book, however, we'll focus in on just a single offer sales funnel so that we can dissect its components. You can add offers later if you'd like, but we'll focus on just one for the sake of simplicity.

In every sales funnel, <u>a business needs to move a person from "interested in" to "committed to" buying</u>. That's not always an easy feat, and, if being fully honest, it's not something that many small businesses even attempt to do. They just leave it up to the customer to make the jump from interested to committed all on their own.

Case in point, not long ago my wife decided that she wanted some new blinds for our house. So, I pulled open a quick search on my phone, found a local custom blind company that had good reviews, and called them out for a free in-home sales consultation. Naturally, my wife was excited about the blinds she was going to get… and I was excited about the sales process I was going to dissect. But that's beside the point.

When the "salesperson" showed up, he quickly introduced himself – a bit nervously, albeit – and then proceeded to walk around the house measuring windows and jotting down dimensions. Once he was all done with that, he went back out to his van and returned with literal suitcases of binders full of samples of various styles, colors, and materials. My wife was filled to the brim with excitement.

Well, after about an hour of humming, hawing, and going back and forth with "this or that" comparisons, my wife had her choice all picked out. "Yippee!", I thought. "He's finally going to *sell* me something". I waited with bated breath.

The salesperson pulled out his pen, grabbed his calculator, and crunched numbers; focusing intently on the deep math he was performing. Then, he did it, he wrote a number on his paper, added a dollar sign, and handed it to me. "There ya go, that's how much it'll cost ya", he said.

I didn't even look at the number. Not because I was afraid of it, but because I was waiting for the sell. The pitch. The variable scoping, variable pricing. The tie-in to emotional motivators. The logical justification. The sense of urgency to act now. The reasons why this was the best option for us based on what we were looking for. The disqualification of any other competitors that we might request a quote from. The reiteration and restating of the reasons why we felt we needed new blinds. The clear directions for what to do next if we want to move forward. *Anything* that might resemble selling.

Much to my dismay, it never came. The guy simply said "Well, I'll leave you two to talk about things and let me know what you want to do." Then he left, without even giving us a card, a phone number, an email, or even instructions for who to contact at the company if we want to move forward. He simply left my wife and me to decide if we wanted to make the jump from "interested in" to "committed to" buying from his company.

Let's be clear here. <u>This was NOT a sales process</u>, it was an *order* taking process. Nothing more, nothing less. It was almost the same level of salesmanship as I receive at the fast food drive through, except they at least upsell me by asking if I want to add fries and a drink!

The thing is, his process wasn't much different from what I see many small businesses do. They have an order taking process, and <u>*not*</u> a process that they use to convert a lead into a long term or high value customer. As such, they miss the mark when it comes to maximizing their sales and making the most of their marketing expenditure. With that background, we can now transition into what a sales process/funnel really looks like and how you can implement one in your business.

At its core, a Sales Funnel is a process that <u>*motivates*</u> a lead to move from "interested in" to "committed to" buying. In order to do that effectively, the sales process needs to have <u>planned</u> elements built into it that instill within the person making the decision:

1. *Belief* that it will work for them, or will satisfy their needs, in their given circumstances.
2. An emotional reason *driving* the purchase.
3. A logical reason <u>*justifying*</u> why they need it.
4. A sense of urgency
5. Belief that they can afford it because the <u>*value exceeds the price*</u>.

6. A clear understanding of what they need to do in order to move forward.

One of my favorite stories that illustrates how this works is from one of my mentors, Russel Brunson, who took a $600 used iPhone, stood on a stage, and in less than an hour had 3 people *legitimately* willing to pay him $750,000 dollars for it. Mind boggling, right? Well, only until you understand *how* he did it.

You see, to most people, an iPhone is an iPhone. There aren't many feature and functionality differences between versions. They are what they are, and they are worth what they are worth. That didn't stop Russel from increasing the value of his through a bit of salesmanship, though.

He started his pitch by telling his crowd the story of how he just got the phone and wanted to be able to access his learning library wherever he went. As an avid business and personal development junkie, he had over 20 years of some of the most expensive courses and trainings ever created saved as audio files on the phone. He had the best of the best from Dan Kennedy, Tony Robbins, Bill Glazer, Ryan Deiss, Napoleon Hill, and many, many more. He had paid over $750,000 for these courses over the years, and whoever purchased the phone would get immediate access to them.

Then he switched gears, opened up his contacts list, and started rolling through some of the people that he had personal contact details for. People like, Tony Robbins, Dean Graziosi, Daymond John, Jenna Kutcher, Prince EA, and hundreds of other top level business leaders, influencers, politicians, actors, musicians, and others. He had spent decades networking in some powerful circles and had made a few friends over the years. And, for anyone that purchased his phone, they would be able to call those people up and say that Russel recommended them to the person. This benefit alone could be worth millions upon millions of dollars to a smart businessperson.

But he didn't stop at that, oh no. Then he pulled open his Voxer messaging channel, an app that he uses to communicate with his personal clients and mentees. It costs each of his clients $50k per year to have this kind of access to him, and anyone that purchased the phone would have access to his Voxer channel forever into to the future.

There were a few other things that he included in the deal just to sweeten the pot, but I think you're starting to get the point here. He sold the phone based on his knowledge of a good sales funnel, *instead* of letting it sell itself based on its basic features and benefits.

To tie things back to the bulleted elements that we covered above:

1. He gave his audience *belief* that if they owned his phone that they could put it to work for them.
2. He convinced them emotionally that having his phone would boost their social status in the world – giving them access to some of the most influential people on the planet.
3. He tied the value of what he was offering back to monetary values so that he could logically justify the price.
4. The total value of what the phone could be worth to the buyer greatly exceeded the price tag, making almost any price seem affordable.
5. He created a sense of urgency/scarcity by saying that there is only one phone, and he would be selling it that night.
6. He instructed his audience on how they could bid for the phone in an auction, giving them a clear understanding of what to do if they want to move forward.

If you take notice, he hit on all 6 of the core elements of a good sales process. Yet, he never even really did what most people consider "selling". He didn't list a bunch of features, benefits, and technical specs. Nor did he use a bunch of hard or high-pressure sales tactics to push his customers to sign on the dotted line. All he did was tell people the story about what was on his phone, what some of those things had done for him, and what they might do for them if they too chose to purchase his phone. He made his audience feel as though they personally could achieve so much more than they had ever dreamed of *if only* they had that phone.

That… is good selling. Effortless, value based, and personal.

So, if you want to maximize your sales through a sales funnel – online or offline – then you need to model this process and use it to **_motivate_** your leads to move from "interested in" to "committed to" buying. Again, to do that effectively, your sales process needs to have planned elements built into it that instill within the person making the decision:

1. _Belief_ that it will work for them, or will satisfy their needs, in their given circumstances.
2. An emotional reason _driving_ the purchase.
3. A logical reason _justifying_ why they need it.
4. A sense of urgency
5. Belief that they can afford it because the _value exceeds the price_.
6. A clear understanding of what they need to do in order to move forward.

Fortunately, there is a framework that you can use that simplifies just how to do this. It is not my own framework, though, so instead of paraphrasing it here, I'll direct you to the resource that best teaches it.

CONTINUED COMMUNICATIONS

Once you've gained a lead through your lead magnet and then run them through your sales process, you'll find that some will buy and become customers… and some won't. This is perfectly natural and is just a reality of the business world. So, don't freak out about it.

Whether a person buys or doesn't buy from you after going through your sales funnel shouldn't really matter to you. I mean, it *does* matter because you want as many people as possible to convert from lead to customer, but it doesn't matter from a lost lead perspective.

Why? Because you never truly lose a lead until one of two things happen: either you stop communicating with them of your own volition, or *they* tell you to stop communicating with them.

So, if you plan to continue your communications with your leads that don't convert to customers on the first go 'round of your sales funnel then it doesn't really matter if they convert or not. You've already spent the money and effort to get them on your list, so you can <u>keep them there until they're ready to buy</u>. It shouldn't really cost you much to continue marketing to them.

You never know when it is that a lead will be ready to transition to a buyer. There are so many reasons for inaction at the time of sale that <u>even perfect sales funnels can convert at seemingly low numbers</u>. People might be genuinely ready to buy, but just have too much going on in their lives at the time they're looking. Or, they might have debt that they need to clear up first. Or, they might be getting married or having a baby that they're a bit nervous about. Again, there are so many reasons – external to your sales process – that you can't worry about their buying decision in a moment. <u>Just keep on marketing to them until they either become a customer or tell you to stop</u>.

I've personally been on a business' mailing list for years before I ever became a customer. I tend to be a slow buyer, going through the full sales cycle and then sitting on the sidelines evaluating the business for months or years before buying. That's just me. I'm analytical, and there a whole lot of people just like me who are the same way. If you don't keep marketing to us over the long term then we'll never become a customer.

Deploying Your Asset Based Marketing

Now that we've covered what asset-based marketing looks like and how to set it up for your business, it'll be time for you to head out and create your own.

In short, this means that you'll begin building a list of leads using targeted advertising and a lead magnet. Once someone is on your list, you'll begin selling to them over and over again by directing and redirecting them into your sales funnel. You'll keep at it until they ask you to stop.

If you do this correctly, your list and your customer based will *both* continually grow, despite whatever economic conditions might be happening around you. That's the beauty of it. When you can consistently and predictably grow despite market conditions then your business will be as close to recession proof as they come.

RECESSION PROOF

PART 2, SECTION 3
Storyselling.

RECESSION PROOF

THE STRATEGY:

The late Gary Halbert, who was one of the best copywriters ever, once said that the most common missing ingredient in sales messages was story. He believed that businesses and professional sellers greatly underutilized the power of story in their sales process, and their results suffered because of it. I tend to agree.

Most businesses focus their marketing and sales around the features and benefits of their products and services. They tell all about what their offerings can do, what it is composed of, why they are so much better than their competitors, and all the cool benefits that people get from what they have to offer. Blah, blah, blah, yada, yada, yada.

People don't *really* care about all those things. Instead, they care about:

1. If they_*believe* that it will work for them, or will satisfy their needs, in their given circumstances.
2. If it fulfills an emotional need or desire that they have.
3. If they can logically justify the purchase.
4. If there is a need for them to buy it right at this moment in time.
5. If it's worth more than what they are paying for it.
6. If they know what they need to do when they are ready to purchase it.

Well, if you remember the story in the last chapter about my mentor, Russell, selling an iPhone for $750,000 then you might remember what it was that set his phone apart from any other iPhone. It *wasn't* the phones features. Nor was it the benefits that the phone created. It was the ***story*** about how and why that specific phone that he was selling would change the purchaser's life, in more ways than one. The stories that he told *created belief* within his buyers that met all 6 of the elements of a good sales funnel.

Often times, the difference between a "blah" sales process and one that absolutely excels in every regard is little more than storytelling. A good story creates connection, offers relatability, and instills a mental image of good outcomes much better than a list of features of benefits ever could.

The "This Is What We Do" Trap.

Most businesses, as in 99% of them, like to tell their prospective customers what they or their product does and that it's the best. "We're XYZ consultants and are the best because ABC", "We sell shoes that are the best because of 123", "We ____ and are the best because ____".

Like clockwork, businesses state what they do and then follow it up with some version of why they are the best. Over and over again, in every industry, they do this. "We're ___, and we're the best."

Well, good for you cowboy/cowgirl, but your customers don't care! Everybody says those things, few believe them.

It is only maybe 1% of businesses that take a different track by telling the stories of how their business came to be instead of telling what it does and why it's the best.

One of my favorite stories of this is of Jaime Cross of MIG Soap & Body Co. who when asked about her business doesn't say "we're a naturopathic soap company and we're better than the off-the-shelf soaps you see at the store." While that might be the technical definition that a business school trained consultant might tell her to lead with, she doesn't.

Instead, she will light up and tell the story of how at church one Sunday in South Carolina, her pastor stopped mid-sermon, placed his hand over his heart, breathed deeply for a moment, and then said "This has never happened to me before, but the Lord just spoke to my heart, and he said that there's a stay-at-home mom in the audience that God wants to give a billion-dollar idea to. So, get ready for it."

She *knew* that the message was for her. And two weeks later, on October 5th, 2010, she awoke suddenly from a vivid dream. A dream set in a giant room in the middle of a stone cottage where she was pouring vats of oil, which were erupting with purple flowers.

She tells how that dream was the catalyst that started her business of crafting handmade soaps with high-quality natural ingredients that are safer, cleaner, and better for your skin than the mass-produced soaps available in stores. Then, she'll shift her story and begin telling you about the people who had skin ailments soothed by her soaps; giving full detail into the pains that the ailment had brought to their lives, and of the relief that the soaps brought.

It's her "origin story", and it alone perfectly sells her soap to her ideal customers, who tend to be Christian stay-at-home moms who are weary of the chemicals in most mass-produced products available at the store and who want only the best for their families. The story creates connection, offers relatability, and instills a mental image of good outcomes. It is _so much_ better than the old "this is what we do" messaging that most businesses use.

So, for your own business, what's your origin story? Is there a story that you can bring forward and tell that will create connection with your buyers, offer relatability, and instill a mental image of good outcomes?

The Story That Adds Value.

Many businesses like to tell their customers about what makes them different from their competitors to help them justify their value and price. For most businesses, a higher price will require more differentiation from competitors; better features, more benefits, more service, etc.

Well, if you're looking for differentiation in your business, you need to look no further than the story that you tell about what you do and how you do it. Not only does your origin story tell of what you do, but other stories can be used to increase the value of what it is that you do.

Don't believe me? Just take a look at MyPillow, BluBlockers, Clickfunnels, Young Living Essential Oils, and a whole range of other products and services that, in essence, are very similar to many, many, other products and services in their respective class. Functionally, they don't have substantial product differentiation.

Aside from maybe Clickfunnels, the others on the list should be commoditized products that sell for about the same value as their competitors… but they aren't, and they don't. They sell for a heck of a lot more than almost anything else on the market, and not just a mere 20%-30% more, their sales prices are closer to 5x-10x of their competitors.

Case in point, everyone knows the value of a pillow, right? Why, then, does MyPillow sell for five times what other "premium" pillows sell for? It's really not much different from other pillows. Arguably, it's not made of any materials that are substantially better than other pillows, and you're not likely to sleep all that much better than you would with other higher end pillows.

So, what is it? Why does MyPillow sell for so much more than its comparable competitors?

The answer is simpler than most realize. It's the MyPillow guy and **_the story he tells_**. If you've never seen the story then I'd encourage you to look it up, deconstruct it, and use some of what he is doing in your own storytelling.

To summarize the story he uses, he starts off by pulling out all of the different types of pillows on the market and then, one by one, pointing out their flaws and calling them useless before tossing them on the floor. Repeatedly throughout his story, he speaks about the ailments caused by poor alignment during sleep and how his pillow uniquely solves the ailments by conforming to each user's unique anatomy. Things like neck aches, numbness and tingling, migraines, tossing and turning, headaches, general fatigue, and other ailments… are all alleviated by his pillow. He then shifts gears and tells of the materials used in, and patented design of, the MyPillow, while highlighting how it's manufactured in the USA.

All throughout his presentation, he infuses stories of users and how in just a matter of nights their ailments began to resolve, allowing them to sleep better, and their lives improved. He offers story after story from people of all shapes, sizes, and ages so that he covers the bases of "they're just like me and it works for them, so it might work for me too."

His collective story and user stories create intrigue and sure sounds a lot better than his competitors' story of "we made this pillow in a 3rd world country, using cheap materials and cheaper labor, and then shipped it across an ocean on a rat-infested ship before selling it to you in an overpriced department store. Oh, and it's probably not going to work with your body type." Okay, maybe that's not the story that they tell, but that's what customers think of when they think of how other pillows are made, and what they do for them, especially after hearing the MyPillow guy's story.

More than anything about his product, his story is what allows him to command higher prices than his competitors. It instills a belief within his customers that <u>it is better and worth more</u> than anything else out there, even though when held side by side with a comparable product, the differences are not *all* that notable (in my personal opinion).

So, when you think of your own business, what story are you telling that makes your products or services seem better and worth more than what your competitors offer? Often times, the biggest difference in value perceived by your customer will be the story that they hear.

Proactiv, The Infamous Acne Glop, Was Built On Story, Not Effectiveness.

In the 90's and early 2000's, I couldn't go anywhere without hearing about this new acne solution called Proactiv. Maybe it was just because I was a pimply faced teen at the time, but the darn stuff was everywhere.

Commercials were running near non-stop. Magazines were filled with full page ads. Moms were telling their friends about how they think the glop might help their teen come out of hiding. It was the talk of the teenage town.

But why? You never really heard about its formula or anything. Nothing about how it was made of ingredients that were so much better than every other glop on the market. And certainly, you never heard about how well it actually worked (since the FDA and FTC don't allow those types of claims to be made).

The reason it took off so well was because the people running its marketing department new something that other acne treatment companies didn't. They knew that story sells. So, instead of telling the market about how great the product was, they told everyone about its radical success stories. Stories like the one of a mom who was worried that her daughter was suicidal because she was so heavily depressed about her severe acne and the social implications of it. After just a few weeks on ProActiv, her depressed teen was happy again.

Or, the story about the mom worried about her daughter not wanting to attend prom who, almost magically, had a pimple free 16 year old emerge from her dungeon happy and excited about a major life milestone instead of throwing an emotional, hormone fueled, tantrum about her "ugly" face.

Or, the story about the two dermatologists who invented the stuff who each had kids who were afraid to be seen in public because of their acne. So, they teamed up and got to work in their lab to develop a miracle cure, and that's what they did.

Starting to see a trend here?

Proactiv's marketing <u>was not about their product at all</u>. It was about the stories of its users and its inventors. Nothing more. Nothing less. Just simple stories of transformation from troubled teen to happy young adult. These stories were geared not towards the teen themselves, but to the real buyers, the moms. It was brilliant marketing that we can all learn from.

That's because...

A Great Story CAPTIVATES Buyers.

It's almost as if stories have the ability to hypnotize buyers, shake them until all sense has left them, and then convince them, subconsciously, that a product or service is worth more than everything else on the market.

That's not by accident.

Story creates immense relatability. Relatability gives customers assurance that "hey, that person is just like me…" which is the most impactful assurance that one can give. So much of a product or service's success is determined by the customer's **_belief_** that it can help them. The more belief, the more sales.

A great story allows you to create the effect where customers think to themselves…

"I Want Your Product, And Don't Care How Much It Costs. I Just Want It Because I Know, Without A Doubt, That It's For Me".

It won't be features and benefits that do this. It never has been. The only thing that creates this thought – and belief – within customers <u>is story</u>.

THE TACTICS:

The Stories You Must Tell

If you're anything like me, leveraging story in your business might seem like a bit of a daunting task. As an analytical person, my natural storytelling approach is mostly limited to "I went over there, did this thing, and then came home. That's it." Stories just aren't in my nature. Like a lot of people (maybe even you), I'm more factual, direct and to the point, and short on the "fluff" that often comes in stories.

For many years, I fought storytelling in my business. I stuck to the facts, kept it short, and always focused on the work. In my head, I thought that good, high-quality, work would speak volumes beyond what any fluff filled story would do.

I was wrong.

Good, high-quality, work is an expectation of a buyer, not a marketing message. You'd never want to run an ad saying something along the lines of "we do good work", because, honestly, people don't care about that. They expect it... but it doesn't connect with them, help them to relate to your business, or instill an image of a good outcome. Only story does these things.

That's why it's imperative that you learn how to weave story into your business – every aspect of it. From your origins and what brought you into business, to your value and why what you do is so much better than anything else on the market, to what your customers think about having done business with you. You need stories for it all, and those stories need to be weaved into how you describe your business and sell your products.

How You Came To Do What You Do

Too often, when I talk with entrepreneurs about why they started their business, I get a version of "I was just born wanting to be in control of my destiny." That's all well and fine, that's a big reason that I'm in business too... but it's not really a reason that most of your customers are going to care about.

What your customers care about is how you <u>earned the ability</u> to be great at what you do, <u>learned the secrets</u> that make you better than most, or <u>came up with the idea</u> that sparked your inventiveness to create what you create. They want to know the situation you were in before you found your calling, the problems that existed that you saw a better way around, and how you came to the point where you put your foot down and said "I'm doing this my way!"

Secretly, people love a good story about someone standing up and fighting against the status quo to do something different. It evokes a feeling of independence in themselves. That's a big reason that most Hollywood movies feature a hero who, in one way or another, stands up against an evil that seems to be rooted in everyday culture. The hero's journey from everyday person to champion of their cause is one that the audience sees themselves in, emotionally connecting them to the plot.

Your business needs to do the same – tell your origin story with you positioned as the protagonist that they can see themselves in.

To embed how and why this concept is so important, let's take a look at one of my favorite superheroes, Batman. Batman, in concept, is a bit of a strange character. He's a grown man who dresses up in an overly tight leather suit and jumps around at night performing random acts of vigilantism. He has no real job, doesn't ever say much, is somewhat of a non-social "loner", and lives in a cave with bats. If I were to describe him in modern day times as a real person, people would be sprinting over to Wayne mansion to get this wacko locked up before he does something weird.

If you were to really think about it, Batman is not much of a likeable character.

That said, when you add in the story about how his parents were murdered in front of him as a child in a crime ridden city overrun with greed and corruption... and then how he was sent away to a place where, stricken by grief, he assumed a new identity and trained for years to become Batman. All of a sudden, he becomes a lot more relatable to the common person. Instead of a wacko in tights, they see him as a crusader of justice similar to what they themselves might have become in similar circumstances.

The story of where he came from, of how he became who he is, makes him human, and helps to make his odd-duck character become likable, trustable, and noble.

Don't get me wrong here, I'm not trying tell you that you need to have an odd-duck character. Rather that a good origin story will help you better connect to your customers, relate to them, and instill a vision of good outcomes in their mind.

Much like Jaime Cross does with her soap business origin story, you can connect at a deeper level with your customers by telling them of the situation you were in before you found your calling, the problems that existed that you saw a better way around, and how you came to the point where you stood up as a champion for your cause.

This is impactful because it explains your business in a way that they can understand without tuning you out as trying to sell them something. They listen, they engage, and they emotionally connect.

The Outcomes You Deliver

The next story that you must curate for your business is one of your customer and, more specifically, the situation they commonly find themselves in before they find you. Much like how in your origin story you want to convey relatability, in your "outcomes" story you want to convey understanding. By telling a story that shows you understand what they are going through, what they have tried, and what they need next, you are able to connect with them at a deeper level.

Let's face it, every person who has ever had a problem in life has tried a few things to solve it. If they have a health condition, they've likely tried all the meds, the common natural therapies, and all the rest without resolution of their symptoms. If they have a challenge in their business, they've likely read the books, hired the consultants, and tried the strategies without breaking through the barrier. If they are looking to build a house, they've likely looked at the inventory of existing homes on the market, considered renovating something else, and looked up a few other builders without finding the right fit for them.

Their problem, and everything they've tried to resolve it, are pain points that you need to hit on in your story by telling of your own experiences trying those exact things. If you haven't tried those things yourself then find a customer spokesperson who has so that they can tell their story of all the things that they tried, unsuccessfully, to solve their problem.

What you're doing here is turning the dagger that causes their pain ever so slightly so that their frustration boils up at the time when you need it to – when you're selling to them. The other thing that you're doing is picking up rocks and throwing them at your enemies. By telling the stories of how your competitors' "solutions" were tried to no avail, you're subtly discrediting them as a viable solution to your customer's problem. This is key to what you do next.

Once you've seeded the idea through story that your competitors' products and services aren't all that effective, or not as effective as your customer would like them to be, or come with negative side effects, it'll be time to tell the story of how you, or your customer spokesperson, tried your product or service and it *finally* solved the problem.

In copywriting, we call this story framework "Problem, Agitate, Invalidate, Solve" and it's quite effective. The gist of it is that you define a problem, agitate and emotionalize that problem through story, invalidate other options they might be considering, and then introduce the new solution as *the* solution to the customer's problem. It's all done through stories that your customers can relate to because they've lived it, they've tried or considered similar things, and they *want* to believe that because it worked for you or your customer spokesperson that it will work for them as well.

Let Customers Sell For You By Telling Their Story

Early in my sales career, I was a go-getter. I'd attend the industry trade shows, prospect like a maniac, and book sales call after sales call. I'd tell the customers about everything that my product or service would do for them, use the stories that would help to get them across the buying threshold, and then close them.

Then, in one single day, everything changed.

I was at an industry trade show working the booth alongside a 20-year veteran seller. This guy was a GOAT (greatest of all time) within the company, consistently selling 2-3x what the nearest top rep sold almost every year. Nobody in the company, not even the CEO, made as much money per year as he did because his commissions were so high. The guy was a legend.

Naturally, I wanted to learn from him, and I wanted to impress him. So, like any good hustle-drunk young salesperson, I began working the floor, finding ways to spark conversation with every person that I possibly could. Then, once I snagged a prospect, I'd call him over to begin selling alongside me.

What he did every time I called him over, though, surprised me. He didn't *really* try to sell at all. He'd just ask a few questions, learn a bit about the situation that the person was in and then he'd say "Oh, I've got just the person for you to talk to." Then, he'd go find someone at the trade show, or would call somebody on the phone, and then would introduce them to the prospect by telling them who they were and how they were once in a similar situation. Then he'd say, I'll leave you two to chat for a bit and will swing back later.

In my eyes, he was *abandoning* the prospect that I had just worked hard to spark up a conversation with. "What the hell!?!", I thought to myself. But, like any good GOAT, he knew exactly what he was doing. And he revealed it to me late in the first day of the show. I won't bore you with all the details but will summarize his strategy here for you.

What he was doing was letting customers do the selling for him. He knew the situations that they were in when they had first come to us as customers, and he knew the results that they had gotten by using us. He also knew that the customers would tell their honest stories about all the ups and downs of their situations, including the ups and downs that were involved with the work that our company did for them. He didn't care that the stories might not be perfect. All he cared about was that the prospect and the customer would share the details about their respective situations. Then he'd step away and watch from afar without making it obvious that he was watching.

When he began to pick up on body cues of either the prospect or the customer indicating that the conversation was nearing its end then he'd swing back over and engage. It was at that point that he'd begin selling, hitting on all the points we talked about back in the Sales Funnel section of this book.

In this lies the lesson of this section, by letting your existing customer sell for you by telling their story, their honest story, you can more effectively lower the guard of your prospect while building up their interest in what you do. Then, when the time is right, you can step in and close the sale without as much objection, skepticism, or resistance from the prospect. The story of your existing customer got them 90% of the way there and you just have to do the last bit to bring them home.

RECESSION PROOF

PART 2, SECTION 4
Tooting Your Own Horn.

RECESSION PROOF

THE STRATEGY:

"It's not polite to brag about yourself." This societal rule has been ingrained in most of us since the times of our childhood. And, for the most part, it's a good rule to follow. People don't like or appreciate braggadocio (boastful arrogance).

They do, however, want to hear about your business' successes. They want to hear how your customers went from a situation similar to what they themselves are experiencing and then got the same result that they themselves want by using your product or service. In copywriting, we call this social proof.

Social proof is one of, if not *THE*, most important components in driving more new customers into your business. It answers questions for prospective customers, creates a sense of relatability, and "proves" that your product and/or service delivers the intended results.

Without social proof, your sales hinge solely on your *word* that what you offer is as good as you say it is.

No matter how much you wink, smile, and offer promises, there will be customer skepticism if you don't have social proof. Customers will assume – often subconsciously – that your product or service is untested and unproven; carrying a certain level of risk associated with purchasing from you. The bigger the price tag, the bigger the risk of purchase. So, unless you're selling $3 tchotchkes in a low-risk sale, they will question the quality of your products and services if you don't have some form of social proof.

That said, social proof rarely just happens on its own. *Most* people – even when they're exceptionally happy with a product or service – don't proactively go out and tell everybody their "before and after" story. They might say in passing or in a random social media post that they like what your product or service has done for them, but this typically only checks a small box on the list of what most prospective customers want to hear.

What is it that prospective customers want to hear?

They want to hear the *story* of the situation the person was in before they found you. They want to understand, and relate to, how the problem they were facing impacted their life. They want to know all the things that they tried before finding you that didn't work. And, last but not least, they want to know what using your product and/or service was like; specifically, what the experience was like, how long it took, what kind of effort (if any) it required, if there were any hidden benefits, and what the outcome was.

There is a lot that prospective customers want to know that most happy customers simply don't share. That's where tooting your own horn comes in (by sharing the stories *for* them).

In order to get these customer stories that offer social proof for your business **you need to grow them, harvest them, and distribute them**. That is the only consistent and reliable way to showcase your business using social proof. As a starting place, there are three types of social proof that you can grow, harvest, and distribute:

- **Testimonials**: A relatively brief (1-3 sentence) statement from a customer whereby they tell of the amazing result they got from your product or service.

- **Case Studies**: A full story of their situation and challenge before they came to you, all the details of what it was like while actively using your product/service, and what the outcome/result they achieved by doing so.

- **Endorsements**: An endorsement from a customer made in the form of a letter, email, phone call, in person discussion, or other communication that is from a customer to a prospect, someone they might know, or someone who otherwise might relate to them (e.g. same role in the same industry). This endorsement is a mini-case study telling of their pre, during, and post situation (and it's what we used in the last section on Storyselling).

Getting Great Testimonials

Having personally received testimonials from legends like Brian Tracy, Bob Proctor, Rodney Reider, and others, I can personally attest to the fact that testimonials don't just happen all on their own. They take time. They take nurturing. And, in what might seem a bit backwards to most, they take writing of them by oneself (in many cases).

When I received a testimonial from legendary personal development and sales author/speaker, Brian Tracy, for my first book, it took some work, and I had to write the first draft of the testimonial myself. Brian's a busy fella, and he's not going to just write testimonial after testimonial for everyone who asks him for one. Why would he? It takes time to write a thoughtful testimonial and he doesn't get anything out of spending that time. So, if I hadn't taken the initiative to write the first draft for him and make it as easy as possible for him to finalize and approve then I doubt I would have ever gotten it.

The same is true for *any* testimonial.

When you go out to ask your customers for testimonials you have to make it as easy as possible for them. That means that you either have to write a first draft for them (typically reserved for big name testimonials) or give them examples of what they might say. By making it easy, and even getting them 80-90% of the way there, you greatly increase your chances of getting a testimonial that is usable in your marketing.

Fostering Case Studies

Taking things up a notch from a testimonial, getting a case study from a customer is extremely important and powerful. A good case study helps fuel your customer driven stories and is an absolute must in any mid to high ticket sales cycle.

Like testimonials, case studies don't typically just happen on their own. They require a lot of work and aren't something that most customers are waiting eagerly to give. Even your best customers can be hesitant to provide a case study because of the amount of work involved on their side.

Typically, to get a good case study, you'll need to start with a customer that you know you helped get a good result and then ask them a series of questions that help bring out their story. After that, you might take pictures, shoot video, record audio, or draft up an endorsement letter (more on that in the next section). All in all, it requires a lot of work for you and your customer alike.

That's why I'm a big believer in incentivizing your best customers for participating in a case study by giving them discounts, free services/products, giving them a gift, or agreeing to do a reciprocal case study for their business (if they're a business customer). In almost every situation I've ever seen, case studies are a give-and-take agreement in which your customers give you a case study in return for something that they value.

Obtaining Customer Endorsements

The golden ticket in social proof, in any industry, is a customer endorsement. Much like a testimonial or case study, an endorsement involves your customer offering up their story about using your product or service. The big difference with an endorsement is that it is more than just the story of why the customer loves your product or service, it is their story _plus_ their pitch encouraging others to use your product or service as well.

One of my favorite examples of an endorsement comes from a client of mine who owns a dental marketing agency. As a marketing professional, she wasn't like her customers. She didn't treat patients, she didn't run a practice, and she didn't have the DDS or DMD credentials behind her name.

If you know much about doctors of any kind, they have a tendency to be somewhat elitist; showing more respect to fellow doctors, and less respect to non-doctors (this is a generalization of course, and there are outliers, but as a whole my experience tells me that it is true). The fact that my client wasn't an industry insider with a medical doctorate degree resulted in a HUGE subconscious barrier to her prospects opening up to work with her. They didn't relate well to her and preferred to stick with what they heard from other dentists... because they were like them and understood their day-to-day challenges.

Fortunately, though, we worked together to forge a secret weapon that would help her get around this obstacle – <u>an endorsement letter</u>.

What we did was have one of her best customers endorse her business by approving a few paragraph endorsement letter that we wrote for them. Part of this approval was that they would agree to allow her to send it out to her prospect list using *their* name and credential as the "from" on the envelope. In return, they would get a credit on services for every mailing that she sent out (services that they would otherwise be paying for).

I'm not going to copy and paste the full endorsement letter here for sake of privacy, but I've rewritten the letter in a very similar way so that you can see what an endorsement message can look like.

"Dear Dr. Dentist,

Like you, I run a dental clinic over in Tucson, AZ. For years, I found that my costs to get new patients were running out of control and I couldn't quite figure out how to 1)cost effectively get them in the door, and 2)keep them within my business for long enough to have the profit margins that I wanted.

I was spending money on consultants that didn't really understand my business and was wasting countless hours of my personal time trying to figure out a solution. Nothing was working.

That is until I found, Georgia D. at XYZ Dental Marketing. Now, normally I wouldn't go around endorsing someone to other Dentists who I haven't personally met, but working with Georgia has absolutely changed my practice, and life, for the better. So, when she asked if I'd be willing to write a forward to a marketing letter that she planned to send to you and a handful of others, I had to say "yes!". I owe her so much, and this letter is the least that I could do.

So, if you're in a similar position to what I was once, then I wholeheartedly suggest that you reach out to Georgia D. at XYZ Dental Marketing. You can give her a call at 555-555-5555.

If you're not quite ready, or want to get a bit more information, then she has this amazing free guide called "The Secret, Almost Backwards, Strategy For Getting Dental Patients Cheaper & Keeping Them For Longer". This was the guide that first got me started with her, and you can grab your own copy at www.XYZDentalMarketing.com/freeguide

Sincerely,

Joe Sarraccino, DDS

ABC Dentistry

Tucson, Arizona

P.S. I don't make a penny for recommending Georgia. She's just done so much for me in my business that I feel compelled to tell others. I hope that you'll feel the same after working with her.

If you look to dissect this letter, you might notice that the opening paragraph is all about creating rapport with the prospect. They've received a letter addressed on the envelope *from* a fellow dentist, so the first line of the letter needs to align with that. "I'm a dentist too!" is what it needs to scream to the reader so that they don't feel duped by sneaky tactics.

Next, the letter touches on a few of the pain points common in the industry and then tells of a few of the things tried, unsuccessfully, to solve the problem – things that the prospect is likely to have tried as well. This is helping to pinpoint on the problems that a solution will later be proposed for, while also gently throwing rocks at a few of the other options available to the prospect.

From there, the letter homes in on introducing the solution, which in this case is Georgia herself. This is a critical component to the endorsement letter, but it's also one that can create a good amount of skepticism in the prospect's mind. "Why would you be sending me this letter endorsing someone I've never met? Heck, I've never even met you!" will be the natural thought that the prospect will have as they read it. So, the letter addresses the objection head on right at the moment that the prospect is likely to think it. By spending a few sentences deflating this objection, the letter brings the prospect into a mode of intrigue.

"I wonder what this person/solution has done for this person to make them want to send me this letter?" is likely to be running through their mind at this point. That is the perfect thought for them to have as the letter then transitions into *the sell* where the message conveyed is "if you're like me, then you might want to…".

Here's the thing, though. For most prospects, the first offer made of giving Georgia a call will be too much. Some will resonate and will call the number provided, but most won't. The first offer was just the setup. The real action that we want the reader to take is in the second offer of downloading the lead magnet (going back to the foundational principle of building a list of leads and customers).

This letter was sent to the prospect *as an advertisement* through direct mail in the form of an endorsement. They haven't yet taken an action that warrants spending selling effort on them, so the letter needs to drive them towards taking that first action. It does this by directing them to the lead magnet (as all advertising should do).

The last part of the letter is the signature block with a quick "P.S." that is intended to restate the objection buster. Skepticism is always the biggest driver of inaction with endorsement letters, so it's a good idea to address it at a few points in an effort to break the objection just enough that it doesn't inhibit action.

Hopefully, this section has illustrated for you what an endorsement is, what it might look like (although they may come in many forms), and how a good one is composed. Again, while it is the customer who an endorsement comes from, 99% of the time it is the business that must craft it. Don't ever expect a customer to put together a phenomenal endorsement for you all on their own. You'll need to do your part to curate and craft it if you want it to be any good. And, as always, if you'd like a little help with this, then swing on over to www.SIMPLsales.com and submit an inquiry to me and my team. Here's the QR code for the site.

THE CLOSING OF PART 2
Sales Truths.

RECESSION PROOF

PART 2 – GROWTH OBSESSION

I am about to reveal my million-dollar truth about new customer acquisition. Well, actually, it's a series of six truths, but who's counting?

Before I do, however, I have a confession to make. I love sales. I mean, I really, *really*, love sales. This isn't just some mild infatuation that comes and goes for me, I'm fully <u>obsessed</u> with sales. I admittedly prioritize it more than other areas of my business, even though I know I shouldn't. It's just how I'm wired.

I spend my days actively selling, my nights actively studying selling, and my weekends writing about my sales experiences and learnings – the good, the bad, and the insightful. My company name is SIMPL Sales for goodness sakes. It's safe to say that I am "all-in" when it comes to sales.

Why this matters to you, and why I'm confessing it, is because if you were to ever meet me… I wouldn't really seem like a salesperson to you. Not in the slightest. I'm somewhat awkward with my words, am a little bit shy and reserved, and overall am not a "salesy" fella. I'm a far cry from the well-put-together, smooth talking, and quick-witted salespeople that normally grace the profession. But that's the beauty of it, I don't need to be like them.

When most people think of sales, they cringe. This is true even of most entrepreneurs. The thought of selling something makes them feel icky inside, so they just don't do it. Much like the window coverings/blinds salesman that I talked about earlier in the book, many entrepreneurs would rather say "this is what I do, and this is how much it costs" and then let their customers move themselves from *interested in* to *committed to* buying. They are perfectly fine not implementing a sales process because they are too afraid of feeling awkward when doing so.

Well, if I may introduce a somewhat uncomfortable idea, how awkward might it be when you have to close your business because a recession hits and your flow of new customers dries up? How awkward might it be when you have to begin submitting applications to jobs that you're well overqualified for, but that you can't seem to get because being an "entrepreneur" doesn't hold weight in the corporate world? How awkward might it be when you fall a few payments behind on your mortgage or car loan and have creditors hounding you for money that you don't have?

I do apologize for being a bit gloomy here, but these are all very real risks that are made incredibly more likely when you don't have a _real_ sales process in your business, especially when a recession hits. The point here is that the awkwardness of failure should scare you a heck of a lot more than the awkwardness of sales.

Remember, I'm not _naturally_ a salesperson, yet I've come to love sales to the point where I am absolutely obsessed with it. From market selection, to lead generation, to conversion, through to ascension, I love it all. And you can too.

You see, I've learned through quite a bit of trial and error that sales doesn't have to feel awkward or unnatural. Nor does it have to feel confusing or overwhelming. In fact, if it does then that is a sign that something is off in the sales process. Sales in your business should feel smooth, easy, and even fun. When it does, you'll come to find your obsession with it, and that's the ultimate goal of this entire section of this book. Because, once you have an obsession with new customer acquisition, then you have a "feeder" of customers that you can become obsessed with… and will have more reliable data points for your obsession with continually improving results. It all comes full circle. And it all starts when new customers are coming into your business.

All that said, I haven't forgotten about the Truths that I promised you here in this closing. In reality, we've already covered the first truth, but we'll lead with it again here:

Truth #1: The Obsessions Are Interlinked

Naturally, every business owner, depending on their personality type, will gravitate to one of the three obsessions critical to business success. Analytical types will more often than not lean towards an obsession over continually improving results, while Relational types more often lean towards an obsession with the customer's experience, and Creative types more often lean towards an obsession with customer acquisition.

There is absolutely nothing wrong with this so long as all three obsessions are held and acted upon. Much like a tricycle will grind to a halt if missing one wheel, so too can your business if missing an obsession. They are interlinked and interdependent. At the same time, new customer acquisition is the wheel that is attached to the pedals; the wheel that delivers inertia, momentum, and direction to the rest of the bike.

Truth #2: Serve Starving Crowds

There is an old story about a business consultant who was running a seminar with a crowd of entrepreneurs and small business owners. During the seminar, the consultant suggested an imaginary scenario for everyone in the audience to ponder on. He said, "Imagine that it is the 1950's and you're about to open a hamburger stand. What is the single thing that will be most important to your success?" Answers quickly came out of the crowd. "Secret sauce", yelled one attendee. "Superior service", yelled another. "A prime location", yelled yet another. The answers kept rolling in, but the consultant disregarded each as good but not quite right. After a few minutes of letting the crowd throw out guesses, one lucky participant stood up and said, "Hungry customers?"

"Ding, ding, ding!", the consultant erupted. "You're right, hungry customers will be the most important thing to your success. Everything else will be *ancillary* to that."

We often times forget this truth in business. We see what it is that we want to do, such as build our own little hamburger stand, but we don't think about who it is that we're going to serve and whether or not they are hungry for what we do. Well, I'm here to tell you, your job as a business owner is to find the crowd that is hungry, or better yet, *starving*, for what it is that you have to offer.

If you can't find your starving crowd then it will be your job to either change what it is that you do so that you have something that has people eager to get it OR _create_ a starving crowd by making what you do in demand. And, yes, you can create demand for what you do.

A prime example of a business that didn't have a starving crowd but created one comes from just down the road from me in Kuna, Idaho, at American Ostrich Farms. Now, you might be wondering what the heck an ostrich farm is and how it makes its money. I mean, this is a business that is located out in the middle of the southern Idaho desert, down a half mile long dirt road, surrounded by acres and acres of nothingness. It's most certainly not a petting zoo (as I would have assumed it was). It turns out, American Ostrich Farms, is a meat ranch, much like those you see with cattle, pigs, chickens, and all the "normal" meats that everyday Americans eat.

If you're wondering who eats ostrich meat then it's safe to say that you're in good company. It's not a common food in most parts of the world, and this proved somewhat problematic for the owners of the farm. They didn't have a starving, or even hungry, crowd when they first started up. So, they had to create one.

Through the use of story, American Ostrich Farms positioned its product, ostrich meat, as a top-tier prime meat that is healthier than other meats and better for the environment. Their target market, high performance athletes and high-end restaurants; people who would be willing to pay nearly $60 for a raw tenderloin cut. By telling stories of athletes who performed at a higher caliber after being on an ostrich diet, they created a market for their product amongst top-tier athletes. Likewise, by telling stories about how much more sustainable ostrich is compared to other meats, like cattle, while also being healthier, they created a market for their product at upscale restaurants that cater to wealthy, health conscious, environment conscious patrons.

The point here is that it is possible to create a starving market for what you do if you need to. Naturally, finding a starving market that is already out there and just needs to be found should be a bit easier, but you have the option of both – finding or creating your starving market.

Truth #3: Small Steps To Big Wins

Humans, naturally, are risk averse; seeking safety, security, *and surety* wherever they can. This is true in every culture throughout every corner of the world. People want to feel as though the decisions they make and the actions they take will protect them from the thing that we all fear the most, *loss*, while propelling them forward towards what we all want the most, *gain*. Said in simpler terms, <u>people want to get something without losing something</u>.

In most cases, the majority of decisions that people make are made because they believe that the chance of gaining something is substantially more likely than the chance of losing something. This is an important concept to understand in sales because it influences *every* buying decision, especially big ones.

In my business as a copywriter and sales consultant, the highest level of service that I can offer my clients is flying out to their office, spending a week dissecting everything that I can about what they offer and what their customers want, and then crafting a series of sales letters, campaigns, and funnels that will serve as their long-term marketing assets that brings in millions of dollars in revenue. This service is my "big win", and I like to think that it's theirs too. But, as you can imagine, the service isn't cheap. I often charge a front-end retainer as well as a percentage of gross sales for every lead and customer that comes in through the funnel.

If I were to walk up to someone who has no-idea who I am and say to them "Hey, I'll craft a sales letter and funnel that will convert millions of dollars in new revenue for you, all you have to do is pay me tens of thousands of dollars and a percentage of gross sales in perpetuity", what do you think they'd say? "Bugger off, you scammer", would be my guess.

Alternatively, if I were to walk up to them and offer them this book as a low-cost, low risk, option to improve their business' performance during tough economic times, they'd be much more likely to take me up on it. Their potential for gain is much higher than their risk of loss, so it's an easy decision. Then, if I serve them in increasingly more valuable ways over time, they will begin to see that I deliver on what I promise and will be more open to spending more and more money with me. I can grow them as a customer from a few dollars on the front end, to $150, to then $1500, then $15,000, then $150,000, and so on so long as I deliver on the outcomes promised. At every step of the way, they see their potential for gain as greater than their risk for loss, so they become more and more willing to trust me at increasing levels of value. When the day comes for me to offer them my "big win" service of sales letters, campaigns, and funnels, they are much more likely to enthusiastically say "Yes!" instead of "Bugger off."

In a nutshell, I've walked them through small steps to my big win (and theirs!).

Alfred Taubman, a famously successful mall developer in America, often spoke at length about this concept, except he called it "Threshold Resistance". According to Taubman, the entrances to retail stores, as well as the window displays of retail stores, could have either low-threshold, medium-threshold, or high-threshold items on display. A low-threshold display at the front of the store would make it easier and more likely for a shopper to enter, where they could then be introduced to medium-threshold and high-threshold items. Conversely, high-threshold items – items that might be more scary or intimidating to customers – placed at the front of the store would make it scarier or more concerning for a shopper to enter, making them less likely to do so.

In the world of malls, foot traffic is everything, so this concept of Threshold Resistance held real weight and had a direct impact on the overall foot traffic that a store would get. In the regular world of business, more generically, Threshold Resistance applies much the same. People will most often come into your business at the low-threshold tier and will then progressively move upwards to the medium-threshold and high-threshold tiers. It's not a foolproof rule, of course, as handfuls of customers can come in and go straight for the high-threshold tier, but the vast majority of customers will move from low to high. As a business owner, your job is to structure your business so that there is the *least level of resistance* in the overall process of customer acquisition and ascension.

Truth #4: Avoid Being "Uncle Tom"

We all know one. Some of us know more than one. You know who I'm talking about, the guy or gal who whenever you see their number pop up on your caller ID, you know that they are only calling to hit you up for either money or a favor. I like to call this person "Uncle Tom", but just because that's how I picture them. For you, you can call them whatever makes sense for you based on your own real-life experiences with your version of "Uncle Tom".

No matter how many times you try to dodge him, he always finds you and puts you in a really uncomfortable position that you'd rather not be in; asking for more than he should, and being incessant about it. Rarely, if ever, does he return the favor (or even return what he "borrowed").

Put in the nicest of terms, he's a pest. An unwelcome visitor that you would happily get rid of if you could. But, in most cases, "Uncle Tom" is family of some sort – your uncle, cousin, brother-in-law, best friend's brother, old friend from elementary school, or some other sort of relation to you – so you can't just tell him to kick dirt. He's "family", and love him or hate him, you can't drop and abandon him.

But family or not, it doesn't change the fact that every time you see his call coming in or his car pulling up the driveway it makes your heart sink as you think to yourself "What does he want this time!?!?" You know from experience that the only reason he's talking to you is because he wants something. It's almost as though he thinks of you as his personal cash register and/or bank of favors.

The funny thing is, when you look at most businesses today and how they treat their prospects and customers, there are a lot of similarities between them and "Uncle Tom". Every time they hear from the business, they hear:

- "Hey, I'm selling this really cool thing. Do you want to buy it?"
- "Give me your email address so that I can send you an endless amount of daily promotions so that you can buy more of my stuff!"

- "Shoot me your cell number so that I can blow up your phone with texts, because, obviously, you're ignoring my emails."
- "I'd like to invite you to an event I'm hosting so that I can hold you captive as I try to sell you more stuff."
- "It looks like it's that time again… please pay your invoice."

Sound familiar? We've all seen businesses doing these things, repeatedly, but rarely do we take a moment to look at our own business and ask ourselves, "Am I an Uncle Tom to *my* customers?" Sadly, we often are. They see our emails, our direct mailers, our social posts, and all the rest and think to themselves, "There he/she goes again, trying to sell me something."

Let's make no mistake here, you MUST sell to your customers. That is a non-negotiable aspect of business. The problem is when you come across to your prospects and customers as only interested in *getting* something from them. Like "Uncle Tom", you can be viewed as asking for too much too often.

Even if you're delivering fair value at every exchange, if you sell too often then you can alienate your customers and become an annoying pest in their lives instead of a welcomed guest. It's a common mistake, and one born out of the nature of business itself. Sales are the lifeblood of any, and every, business, and every good entrepreneur must keep the blood flowing to keep the business alive and healthy.

Dan Kennedy, the legend of marketing who I've mentioned many times throughout this book, often says that a business must intentionally find its own unique way of being the "welcomed guest" in their prospect's and customer's homes. Becoming the annoying pest can happen quickly, so a business must proactively get ahead of it so that instead of customers thinking "Oh, *him* again" when they hear from you, they think, "He's here! He's here!".

Believe it or not, this is not as hard as you might think. All it takes to become a welcomed guest is two-fold:

1. **Be of constant service to your prospects and customers**; providing simple forms of help, information, advice, or other forms of no-expectation, no ulterior motive, support to them in between your sales pitches.

2. **Create a two-way relationship with your customers**; making them feel as though you have a personal interest in their success with your products/services, and life in general, while also sharing the stories of your life with them.

The challenge for most businesses is doing these two things *at scale*. It's easy enough to do these things for a small handful of top-level customers, but for *all* customers and prospects it can become more difficult. That doesn't make it impossible, though. The answer to service and relationship *at scale* is:

1. **Information marketing**: sharing helpful information products like quicksheets, training, guides, explainer videos, and other tips, tricks, or secrets that are relevant to your customer or prospect.

2. **Relationship marketing**: sharing of information and stories that help make customers and prospects know, like, and trust you, while also doing periodic personalized check-ins.

Through these two types of marketing you can position your business as the welcomed guest that customers know, like, trust, *and* get excited to hear from.

Truth #5: Unquestioned Access To The Keys

I grew up in a small town in Canada and can attest that the stories are true. Not only did we sleep with our doors unlocked, but everything was open to friends, family, and neighbors… everything. There were many times where we'd wake up to an empty driveway, with vehicles gone and fresh tracks through the snow. We didn't call the cops, nor did we bat an eye about it. We just figured that someone we knew needed to borrow it that morning and held solace in the idea that they'd bring it back before we needed to leave. And sure as the sun comes up each morning, they'd bring it back just in time for us to leave, tank filled up and ready for us to roll out.

Most everyone in the town had been given the rights to the keys of what we owned, and us theirs. If someone needed something they were free to open up our front door, rummage through our keys hanging there within arm's reach, and borrow it. Vehicles, ATVs, motor home, tools, toys, and most everything else were all fair game for them to borrow. When they did, they took care of it and returned it in the same or better condition. If something went wrong, they righted it. They were trustworthy, so they were given a near unlimited amount of trust.

Thinking back about this now, and after having lived in places like Los Angeles, Seattle, Jacksonville, Sacramento, and Santa Fe, it seems unreal that the kind of place that I grew up in ever existed at all. In today's world, almost regardless of where you live, trust is very rarely given to anything or anyone. Even many spouses and immediate families struggle to trust each other.

This creates a challenge for many small business owners, as all sales, and I repeat, *all sales* require a certain level of trust. Customers must trust that they will get the outcome that they seek for a fair price that is based on the value delivered. In other words, <u>trust is the key</u>.

If you want the keys to endless success, especially during tough economic times, <u>you must be trustworthy as a business and as a person</u>. The more trust that you can build with your customers, the less you will need to "sell" your customers on anything. They'll simply trust that you know best and will do what is right by them. You'll be worthy of their business, and both you and they will be confident in the worth you deliver.

Truth #6: Success In Sales Is A Habit

Aristotle once said, "We are what we repeatedly do. Excellence then, is not an act, but a habit." Even after thousands of years, this truth still applies to most everything that we do. We become excellent at what we do repeatedly, and mediocre at what we do intermittently.

In business, this truth applies across the spectrum, but, arguably, applies most directly to new customer acquisition. If we are not habitually obsessing over how we will serve a growing number of customers then, at best, our business will be mediocre at bringing new people in. Mediocrity in this area is unacceptable. The competition for new customers is fierce, and it only increases during tough economic times when there are fewer active customers in most industries. A failure to be excellent could very well be the cause of an overall business failure.

It is for this reason that I, again, make the plea for you to become obsessed, in every meaning of the word, with growing the number of customers that you serve by implementing the strategies and tactics shared in this chapter. "Proofing" your business for a recession will undoubtedly begin at this step, as it is the wheel, equipped with pedals at the front of the tricycle, driving your business forward.

RECESSION PROOF

CLOSING
The Recession Proof Framework

RECESSION PROOF

Congratulations! You've made it, and as I said at the start of this book, you are smarter than the average squirrel in the forest.

As other squirrels (entrepreneurs) around you will undoubtedly get "squirrelly" soon, if they aren't already, you now have the blueprint for creating a business that is resilient to market forces imprinted in your brain. You have everything you need at your fingertips. What you do from here, however, will be completely up to you.

If you're like most, you'll begin implementing against some of the ideas shared in this book… but will slowly begin feeling a bit "squirrelly" like the others around you. Fight this with all of your being. Only the smartest, most determined, squirrels in the forest of business will survive the upcoming winter. I want for you to be one of them, and the way for you to do that is to become obsessed with your customer's experience, with your new customer acquisition process, and with your business' continually improving results. These three obsessions must become the drivers within your business.

That said, I know that it can be hard to follow along and implement across the span of 200 pages or so. There is a lot that we covered in this book and having a condensed framework for what to implement and when is typically helpful. That's why we'll close this book out with a recap of what we've covered, but in an order of priority for what to implement and in what order.

So, here we go…

Action #1: Find Out Exactly Who Your Best Customers Are

Let's face it, some customers are great for your business and some customers are absolute headaches. Knowing who is who, and intentionally targeting them in a way that attracts them, and only them, is imperative to not only enjoying your journey as an entrepreneur but also to your ability to 1)convert sales at a higher level and 2)build raving fans within your business who resist patronizing anyone but you, knowingly and willingly pay you higher prices, and provide unsolicited referrals.

__Who__ you serve might just be the most important aspect of your entire business, so it makes sense to really home in on who it is that will be your best customers so that you can build your business around them. From there, you'll have the opportunity to find or create your starving crowd.

Action #2: Create Your Marketing Assets

Good marketing is not a verb. This is a concept that, by this point in the book, should be well established in your mind. While marketing activity is not necessarily a bad thing, it must always point back to your marketing asset(s) that enable you to build a healthy list from a starving crowd using a lead magnet so that you can incrementally sell to those who have raised their hand by using a sales funnel (process) infused with stories and social proof (Phew! That was a mouthful of a sentence. Go back and read it again if you want to pick up on everything laid down…).

Action #3: Deliver A Customer Experience Unlike Any Other

Your customers cannot be indifferent to your business, they must be enthusiastic about it. Creating customers that are enthusiastic all boils down to the experience that they have, especially from the first purchase they make. That's why it is imperative that you "wow" them with an exceptional pre-sale buying experience, keep them engaged and happy through any waiting period between purchase and final delivery, and then shock and awe them post-delivery.

If you establish processes that ensure these things happen, along with the few other tactics shared in Part 1, Section 3, then you will root out customer indifference and build an enthusiastic following. This will allow you to take advantage of one of the most unique advantages in business – retention and ascension of customers (up to ~97.3% of them based on the math).

Action #4: Become "Known" To Your Customers

While this step is snuggled in here at #4, it really is one that should be interwoven throughout all steps. But alas, I wanted to call it out specifically and on its own because it is an important aspect to all other steps. Your prospects and customers must know, like, and trust you. The best way for them to achieve this is to let them get to know you... as a real live person that they can relate to and look to as a leader in your respective market.

Action #5: Become Resilient By Making Raving Fans Out Of Your Customers

When it comes to recessions, resiliency is the name of the game. The business that is most resilient to the external pressures of a down economy will be the winner. Essentially, this means that the business that has the most raving-fans as customers will outshine the rest on both their top and bottom line numbers.

To define a raving-fan, these customers are the ones who:

1. Are <u>unwilling</u> to give your competitors a chance because they are *emotionally invested* in your business.
2. Willingly <u>pay you higher prices</u> because they believe that they get more value through you.
3. Have a compelling desire to <u>tell others about your business</u>.

While these customer attributes are built all throughout your business model, one of the best ways to solidify customers as raving fans is to implement a membership structure that gives them a *compelling* reason to be faithful to your business because of the perks they get. They should have a desire to be *exclusive* with your business because they get more service, status, or other benefits through you than they couldn't otherwise get from your competitors.

Action #6: Stay "Connected" Through Print

As covered in the closing of Part 1, people today are yearning for quality, for service, and for the feeling of connection that they had back in the 90s and 2000s. Put more simply, people realized that they want the ease of the digital economy with the *connection* of the service economy that existed prior to the internet age. They want the best of both worlds, and they are willing to pay higher prices for it.

That said, it is assumed that in your business you have, or easily can, connect digitally with your customers. That's just a given. But that's not enough to create a real <u>relational</u> connection with them. Digital is "cheap", and people today don't want to feel as though the businesses that they "connect" with view *them* as "cheap". They want to feel as though they are valued.

A print newsletter, given the few dollars that it costs to send to a customer, is one of the best investments that you can make in showing your customers that <u>they matter to you</u> and you value their business. In short summary, a good newsletter allows your business to:

1. Remain in consistent contact with your customers in a format that is the most likely to be retained, read, and remembered.
2. Give your customers a deeper sense of "knowing the owner".
3. Keep them up to date on developments in your business, and what might be coming up that they can be excited for.
4. Indoctrinate them on the benefits of your business over others in the market.
5. Market to them for free, or at low cost; subtly introducing upsells and cross-sells.
6. Obtain more referrals to their family, friends, and associates.
7. Enhance their feelings of connection to your business.
8. Reduce objections and resistance to your offers so that you can increase conversions.

For these reasons, and more that we covered in Part 1, Section 3, a print newsletter is a powerful tool for customer retention and ascension that smart business owners can and should use.

Wrapping It Up

Well, we've made it to the end. The real finish line.

We've covered both in detail and in summary the framework for recession proofing your business. We've laid out the action steps, shared the obsessions, and covered all the reasons for which you should implement against them.

Of the reasons to act, and act now, none quite compare in level of concern as commoditization. Commoditization in the coming years will wreak havoc for most small businesses. As consumer and business buyer demand decreases, there will be downward price pressures that erode margins and force businesses into a frenzy in order to keep up with the sales quantity that they need in order to survive. But many won't (survive).

For your business to survive, you must position your business model for quality over quantity. That's not to say that quantity can't still come, but that your business can't be *reliant* on it (as most are). You must make yourself immune to the pressures of commoditization by implementing the strategies shared in this book to make what you do, and what you offer, unique in the marketplace and resistant to price comparison.

Gary Halbert, the world-famous copywriter that I mentioned earlier in this book, once said that almost all other copywriters he knew were in the copywriting business… but he wasn't. He was in the Gary Halbert business; meaning that he didn't compete against the others, he created demand for himself that was independent of external market pressures that might be created by others in his industry.

In that lies the lesson, <u>you must be in the business of you… and *not* what you do</u>. This book will help you to do that.

The rest is up to you…

RECESSION PROOF

A Short Background
About The Author

RECESSION PROOF

About the Author

JASON BARRY is a decent writer, not too shabby entrepreneur, okay speaker, has-been athlete, and super awesome dad and husband. He's proud to have nailed at least one thing in life.

His witty and descriptive style of writing is both fun and easy to read; almost as if he's turning on an old movie projector to bring newfangled motion pictures to the words in his old-fashioned books. Regardless if he's writing about his adventures in raising three wild animals who were born in a litter (triplets), his business escapades working as a globe-trotting consultant for the mob (Fortune 500 companies), or his struggles in trying to keep up with it all (just reality), he tells his story in a way that you can feel the same as he felt in the moment of experiencing it. You can learn the lessons that he learned almost as if you'd experienced them yourself.

In addition to his writing, Jason has spoken on the stage of some big names, live streamed talks to 118 countries, and scored a wife who is *way* out of his league. He's had some huge successes and some soul crushing failures… but has emerged triumphantly both from having his head in the clouds with self-pride (arrogance) as well as being buried under the soils of his losses (self-pity). These days, he tends to coast between the two extremes.

In his day-to-day life, he's the kind of guy who'll drop what he's doing on a moment's notice and fly half-way across the country if you need him (yes, he's done that). He holds doors for people. He shovels his neighbor's driveway when it snows. He awkwardly says "Hi" to all the people he walks by on the street (he's originally from Canada, give him a break). Sometimes, he even wears a cape (for his kids, of course).

He wrote this "about" section himself (conceited)… and hopes that its playful tone in what's supposed to be a serious-but-brief section brought at least one smile to your face. He has terrible humor, but people seem to still smile at him nonetheless (sympathy smiles).

In person, he tends to be pretty bland… so he'll take that smirk on your face right now, any smirk at all, as his sign that he's able to be at least somewhat interesting in this life.

But aside from all of that, Jason is the creator of the SIMPL Marketing System and the Recession Proof Business Framework. He's also the Managing Principal Consultant at SIMPL Sales & Marketing, a consultancy specializing in sales copywriting and conversion systems.

To learn more about Jason, head on over to www.SIMPLsales.com. He might just have a gift waiting for you if you do 😊 .

RECESSION PROOF

References, Resources, & Sources of Inspiration

Brunson, Russell, *Dotcom Secrets*. United States: Hayhouse, 2020

Buck, Shaun, Stop Losing Customers. Lexington, KY: Newsletter Pro, 2019

Carnegie, Dale, How To Win Friends & Influence People, New York: PocketBooks, 1936

Dib, Allan, The 1-Page Marketing Plan. Miami, FL: Friesens Press, 2018

Halbert, Gary, *The Boron Letters*. Los Angeles, CA: Bond Halbert Publishing, 2013

Hill, Napoleon, *Think and Grow Rich*, Meriden, Conn.: The Ralston Society, 1937

Kaufman, Josh, *the personal MBA – master the art of business*, New York: Penguin Group, 2012

Kennedy, Dan, *Magnetic Marketing*. Charleston, SC: ForbesBooks, 2018

Kennedy, Dan; Buck, Shaun, *No B.S. Guide To Maximum Referrals & Customer Retention*. Irvine, CA: Entrepreneur Press, 2016

Kennedy, Dan, *The Best Of No B.S. The Ultimate No Holds Barred Anthology*. Irvine, CA: Entrepreneur Books, 2021

Singal, Anik, *eSCAPE – The 4 Stages Of Becoming A Successful Entrepreneur*, Rockville, MD: Lurn, Inc, 2018

Taubman, Alfred, *Threshold Resistance: The Extraordinary Career of a Luxury Retailing Pioneer*. New York, NY: HarperCollins Publishers, 2007

The Push, Directed by Derren Brown. Performances by Derren Brown, Netflix, 2018

Warren, Rick, *The Purpose Driven Church*. Grand Rapids, Mich.: Zondervan, 1996

www.ingramcontent.com/pod-product-compliance
Lightning Source LLC
Chambersburg PA
CBHW060541210326
41519CB00014B/3299